THE VERY BEST OF
FESS
HOLE

First published in Great Britain in 2022 by Radar,
an imprint of

Octopus Publishing Group Ltd
Carmelite House
50 Victoria Embankment
London EC4Y 0DZ
www.octopusbooks.co.uk

An Hachette UK Company
www.hachette.co.uk

Distributed in the US by
Hachette Book Group
1290 Avenue of the Americas
4th and 5th Floors
New York, NY 10104

Distributed in Canada by
Canadian Manda Group
664 Annette St.
Toronto, Ontario, Canada M6S 2C8

ISBN 978-1-80419-037-1

A CIP catalogue record for this book is available from the British Library.

Printed and bound in Great Britain

10 9 8 7 6 5 4 3 2

All images: Internet Archive Book Images

This FSC' label means that materials used for the product have been responsibly sourced

THE VERY BEST OF
FESS
HOLE

BRITAIN
CONFESSES
ANONYMOUSLY

Rob Manuel

RADAR

*This book
is dedicated to
Pope Francis
and
Simon Le Bon*

Contents

'On the whole, human
beings want to be good,
but not too good, and
not quite all the time'

George Orwell

Introduction

I've always been obsessed with funny stories. Me and my friends turn life into anecdotes to amuse each other, because real life is funny – far funnier than any fiction.

If you're anything like me, there's always an inner voice commenting on your life, going, 'Ooh, that's a bit of a story, I'll tell that to someone.' I'll give you an example. My son Stanley was four years old and we were visiting the Science Museum. At the bottom of the building, there's a water exhibit where the kids can play with dams and mini water wheels. It teaches them hydraulics or something sciencey – but more importantly, kids just like mucking around with water and getting wet. To help control exactly how damp the kids get, the museum offers the use of small yellow plastic cagoules.

So there's my child, with short brown hair and a yellow mac, and I'm keeping an eye on him – and also, if I'm honest here, checking the news on social media and looking up every 30 seconds to make sure he hasn't drowned. Then I spot something on his head. I'm looking down at him from behind, at his brown hair and yellow coat, and there's something odd in his hair. Maybe it's a bit of food; you know how kids are. With my parental monkey-grooming instincts, I reach down to pick at the gunk in his hair, wondering what exactly it is.

Then there's a man in my face: 'Get your hands off my daughter!' I pull my hand away in alarm and look at the shouting man, and then back at my son.

It isn't my son. Same short brown hair. Same height. Same yellow coat. But it's a little girl. And that thing in her hair, that's no dinner residue: it's a bone-anchored hearing aid attached to her skull. So from the point of view of this man, I am a weird stranger interfering with his daughter's hearing aid. I try to apologise and the man is all, 'I don't care. Get away from my daughter.'

2

I leave the Science Museum in shame and humiliation, but a little voice within is saying, 'Well, that's a bit of a story that'll make my friends laugh.'

People often ask me how Fesshole came to be, and essentially it was because I once started a Twitter account about sharing terrible opinions and my friend Pete said to me, 'That's the best Twitter account you've ever made.'

'Is it?'

'Yes. I used to love the internet. I used to be able to moan and nothing went viral. I could complain about my job, about my wife, and only a few weirdos on a forum would read it. I miss the old, slightly anonymous, internet.'

That's when something went *ping* in my head: what if I combined my love of horrible but funny real-life anecdotes and Pete's desire to moan without getting into trouble? Well, you'd get Fesshole, wouldn't you?

So please enjoy these confessions people have sent me, the ones that have done the best numbers on the account and also the ones that make me personally giggle.

And Pete, do please keep moaning; your complaints are the fuel that powers everything.

Let us begin...

First Commandment

Thou shalt

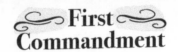

FOLLOW ADVICE

submitted by

the readers of

Fesshole

Imagine Take a Break *magazine if the editors were on crack and the readers were on crack, too.*

Fesshole is here to advise you to live your life better.

Please note: If you try these tips and things turn out badly, send your complaints to tips@takeabreak.co.uk

Someone fly-tipped a bag containing Amazon packaging with their address on it in a local beauty spot. I re-packaged selected items and popped them in the post box without a stamp. They will need to visit the depot to collect their rubbish and pay postage. Hi Gordon, you've got mail.

RT: 339 AV: 5,950

When I'm struggling to edit down to a word count, I hyphenate all the words in a sentence and then make the font colour of all the hyphens white. It looks like a sentence but is only counted as one word. A trick that has helped me many times.

RT: 854 FAV: 5,691

When visiting New York, the wife and I had a routine each night when we ate out: I'd 'propose' to her and she'd tearfully accept. Americans being Americans would whoop and cheer and occasionally the restaurant let us eat for free. We'd been married 8 years.

RT: 843 FAV: 26.7K

Somebody owed me £100 and ignored me for months even when I chased them. So I did a laugh emoji on a status when their dog died. They popped up irate, but they still popped up, and I got the money back.

RT: 47 FAV: 3,944

Every year I sign up to as many cash fantasy football leagues as I can through friends, family & colleagues. I then pay £24 a year to follow an expert on Patreon and copy his team and transfers exactly each week, and end up winning each league. I'm set to make over £4,000 this season...

RT: 239 FAV: 467

When we're in the cinema waiting for the film to start, I use my phone to book the seats around, next to and in front of us – you can book loads of seats & it holds them for 10 minutes without having to pay. No one obscures our view and no annoying kids end up sitting near us.

RT: 220 FAV: 1,663

I did jury service recently. Even though I was certain of the man's guilt, I pretended to be unconvinced during deliberations. This meant no majority and I got an extra 2 days off work before we were eventually dismissed. Not sorry.

RT: 135 FAV: 2,272

Whenever there's a generic discount code on a website like 'discount25', I always try other codes like EventVIP or Discount50. Today I'm heading to a festival with 50% off. Not even sorry.

RT: 97 FAV: 4,074

If one of our children gets invited to a birthday and I don't like the parents, I make sure the present we give is something messy like Play-Doh or kinetic sand. Makes me happy to think about the twat mum/dad clearing it up.

RT: 203 FAV: 3,637

When going to supermarkets, I first hide a 2-litre bottle of soft drink behind the frozen vegetables in one of the freezers. I then retrieve my nicely chilled bottle at the end of my shop. No way I'm spending twice as much for only 500ml just to have a cold drink on the way home.

RT: 406 FAV: 7,048

As a special treat to myself on my birthday, I requested £1 from all my contacts on Monzo. This included ex-girlfriends and people I hadn't spoken to for years, just to see who would pay. I got £11. It was the best day.

RT: 76 FAV: 3,749

My dad is a staunch Tory voter, and doesn't see the need for foodbanks – thinks they stop people from helping themselves. When I do his shopping, I always buy something for the food bank on his behalf and donate to the trolley on the way out.

RT: 1,365 FAV: 33.4K

When my kids were little, they were
fascinated by the vacuum cleaner and
asked if they could do the hoovering.
I told them I'd only let them if they tidied
up first. For ages they thought being allowed
to hoover was a reward for tidying up.

Cooking With Fesshole

Here are some delicious recipes and tips to cook up a delicious treat at home, the Fesshole way.

~~~~

About an hour after breakfast I saw a bit of marmalade on my jumper. I picked it off and put it in my mouth. Sadly, it was jelly from the cat food.

RT: 410 FAV: 8,212

I got curious and stuck a carrot up my arse. Then panicked and thought my parents would notice the missing carrot, so returned it to the cupboard. We ate it for dinner that night.

RT: 34 FAV: 148

Whenever my wife is out of the room, I lick the Himalayan salt lamp that she bought. I absolutely love it.

RT: 193 FAV: 2,692

I have just mistaken a Dreamie for a stray crisp and eaten it. They aren't as tasty as cats make them out to be.

RT: 274 FAV: 4,929

I had a dinner party last weekend that I cooked for. The sauce need grated carrot, but the grater was in the dishwasher mid-cycle. So I chewed up three carrots in my mouth and spat them into the frying pan. A fair bit of chewing, but I think it gave a better texture.

RT: 22 FAV: 1,820

I always make the effort to check the Calpol is still OK before giving it to the little one. It's not really because I feel like checking it, but because the pink elixir of life is delicious.

RT: 117 FAV: 2,393

Accidentally made my morning cuppa with gravy granules. So much nicer. A hot cup of Bisto is far superior to Nescafé.

RT: 260 FAV: 2,498

I've eaten mayo on toast for dinner on more than one occasion. I'm a chef in a 2 Michelin star restaurant.

RT: 73 FAV: 2,783

Cooking for a girlfriend when I was younger, I found some green herbs at the back of her kitchen drawer, smelled lovely. I presumed it was oregano. It wasn't. The bolognese tasted really good, but we had to crawl to the sofa about an hour later.

RT: 45 FAV: 2,507

I made my gf a cheesecake that she loved. It wasn't till the next day I found out I'd made the base from her dog's biscuits. Didn't have the heart to tell her. She's asked me to make it for her mother coming over next week. The in-laws hate me. I'm at the pet shop now to restock.

RT: 466 FAV: 12.4K

Dating Tips

~~~~~~

Want to improve your chances on the dating apps? Here's the Fesshole knowledge, hard won, from the dating scene to help you score big.

~~~~

Sometimes I match my roommate with a fake Tinder account and agree to come over, so that he will clean the apartment. When it's clean, I then cancel.

RT: 697 FAV: 7,878

I once met a girl on a night out. She stayed the night at mine, but in the morning I couldn't remember her name. So I took her to Starbucks for a coffee.

RT: 225 FAV: 4,030

When I have a date with a new guy, I suggest getting steak and order it well done to see if he tries to tell me not to. If he does, I don't see him again – it's been a good asshole-filter for years and I regret nothing.

RT: 322 FAV: 11.2K

After a stagnant couple of months on Tinder, I have decided to take a new approach. I just subtly imply I'm a drug dealer. My shag/match ratio has gone through the roof. I'm not even a dealer, I'm a chartered accountant.

RT: 108 FAV: 2,391

I once went on a date with a guy. I didn't really fancy him, but he told me he had a dog. I love dogs. So I went back to his house just so I could meet the dog.

RT: 101 FAV: 2,827

I have Tinder for the sole purpose of whining to men about my shitty life and boyfriend. Won't shag 'em, but no man could be a more kind, patient, supportive listener than a bloke who thinks he might get his knob wet.

RT: 166 FAV: 2,598

I've got a fake Tinder account where my profile picture is a pig just so I can browse the local talent. The worst part is I've got far more matches with the pig than I ever did with my face.

RT: 83 FAV: 3,084

Dietings Tips
(Do the Opposite to Lose Weight)

*Many people struggle with their weight. The solution is to
live on the Moon, where things weigh less.*

**My girlfriend used to get on my tits about my weight
whenever I mentioned hamburgers. So I started telling
her instead that I'd had a 'beef salad roll' for lunch.
She congratulated me every time for making a healthy
choice, and never did work it out. Not sorry.**

RT: 135 FAV: 3,985

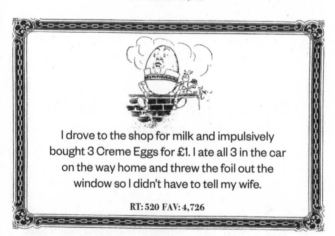

I drove to the shop for milk and impulsively
bought 3 Creme Eggs for £1. I ate all 3 in the car
on the way home and threw the foil out the
window so I didn't have to tell my wife.

RT: 520 FAV: 4,726

**When we have steak in garlic butter for dinner – a rare
treat – I'll tell my wife I don't want any help cleaning
up afterwards and send her off to go relax. Then I take
some bread and use it to eat all the lovely burnt garlic
butter in the bottom of the pan without judgement.**

RT: 101 FAV: 2,314

My wife is 4' 11" and cannot see the top shelf in the cupboard, let alone reach it. That's where I hide the bourbons and that's why I'm not losing weight, despite the diet she's put me on.

I always grate extra cheese when I'm cooking so I can stand there and just eat it all.

My wife thinks I'm still working my way through my Christmas Toblerone. The thing is, I keep replacing it when I'm three-quarters of the way through. I wonder how long I can keep this up.

Dieting Tips (Sincere Advice That'll Actually Work)

Are you struggling to lose weight? Here are some tips to help shed the pounds (other than eating rancid pork).

My wife & I went to Slimming World a few years ago. Lost a ton of weight. Won Slimmer of the Week several weeks, Man of the Year, Couple of the Year, the lot. Everyone was always asking how we managed it. Cocaine. We took loads & loads of cocaine.

Signed up to Slimming World. On my first weigh-in I placed my mum's brass weights in my bra and pockets. Weighed next week, lost a stone, Slimmer of the Week, got a basket of free food, hailed a slimming celebrity and had to explain my diet plan, which they all followed for months.

RT: 291 FAV: 3,115

Shit Science Experiments for You to Try

'Your scientists were so preoccupied with whether they could, they didn't stop to think if they should.' – Jurassic Park

~~~~

I was once curious to find out what happens when the shit hits the fan. Tried it. Don't try it.

RT: 210 FAV: 2,348

At primary school, I took a shit into the urinals to see what would happen. Turns out it just sits there and festers all day.

RT: 42 FAV: 1,375

**I always wondered what it would feel like to poo
in the sea. So I did said deed where no one was around.
Unbeknown to me, a couple of yards away,
a snorkeller emerges from the surface. They turn to me.
Their look of judgement still haunts me to this day.**

Impromptu Games We Play in Public

~~~~~~

*One of the joys of life is making up little games to play
to relieve boredom. A favourite of this editor's is to
keep his eyes peeled for Harold Shipman lookalikes.
There's a lot of 'Shipalikes' about if you start looking.*

~~~~

**When I fill up with petrol, I always try and land the
counter on an exact round number, like £20.00.
If I overshoot by a couple of pence, £20.02, then
I always put in a few pounds more to take it up to
a 'random' number like £23.47 so the cashier
won't know I tried and failed.**

If I'm bored at social occasions, I'll start introducing myself
as having been the bassist in Starsailor. Nobody remembers
what they looked like, so it's believable, and I'll then go on to
make up stories to make the singer sound a right cunt.

**When I'm on the bus and it's approaching my stop,
I test my core strength by not holding on to the pole and
seeing if I can balance standing up until the bus stops.
Sometimes I need to adopt a surfing stance to do it.
I probably look ridiculous, but it's my challenge to myself.**

RT: 262 FAV: 5,336

My wife and I have a game we play when driving.
When one of us farts, they mentally count how long it takes
for the other to smell it. We have two kids now who also
participate. It's the highlight of any road trip.

RT: 62 FAV: 2,658

**There used to be a woman whose walk-train-walk
commute was almost identical to mine.
She was a crazy-fast walker and for a bit I used
her as a pacemaker for increasing my own speed;
I always lost. I now realise this wasn't as subtle as
I thought and would've seemed really creepy.**

RT: 40 FAV: 2,213

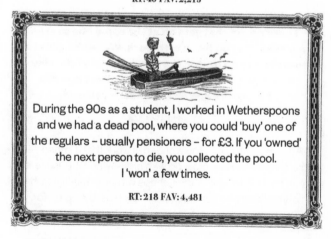

During the 90s as a student, I worked in Wetherspoons
and we had a dead pool, where you could 'buy' one of
the regulars – usually pensioners – for £3. If you 'owned'
the next person to die, you collected the pool.
I 'won' a few times.

RT: 218 FAV: 4,481

When I'm in a shopping centre, I'll pick someone ahead of me as my opponent for a walking race. They're obviously oblivious but sometimes, once I overtake at an unnecessary pace, they speed up too. But they have no chance, the afterburners go on and I'm gone. Victorious.

RT: 110 FAV: 2,551

When I'm entering my PIN, I pretend to enter other numbers on the off-chance someone's got a camera on me so they can't steal my PIN. Doing little feints like I'm the Messi of the chip and PIN world.

RT: 99 FAV: 2,290

There's a girl that gets off at the same bus stop as me every day on the way to work. When she goes to press the button to stop the bus, I wait until she almost touches it and then beat her to it. I've done this for 5 years and she still hasn't realised.

RT: 282 FAV: 7,858

After reading about the wonderful work that Timpson – the shoe-repair people – do with employing ex-prisoners, I can't walk past one of their shops without imagining what crime the bloke behind the counter was locked up for.

RT: 263 FAV: 4,632

When I'm driving on the motorway, I award myself 1 point per wheel every time I change lanes without going over the studs/cats' eyes. I'd got to my high score of 121 points when some twat beeped at me and broke my concentration.

RT: 77 FAV: 2,160

When walking behind people, I pretend I'm a race car in their slipstream and overtake at the last moment to get the most benefits from the low air pressure.

RT: 93 FAV: 2,707

When I see a plane in the sky, I guess the airline, departure and destination before checking on Flightradar24. If I get all 3 right, I treat myself to a pint.

RT: 298 FAV: 4,024

How to Make Money Fast

~~~~~~

Follow these tips – it's a better idea than buying NFTs of bored apes.

~~~~

I'm a reasonably well-known author. I like nothing more than buying my own books for £2 on eBay so I can autograph them and sell them at a profit.

RT: 182 FAV: 2,916

Advice

I'm an Irish speaker in a very loyalist part of Norn Iron. Back in uni, I used to write to my local council anonymously and request government documents be translated to Irish, which they had to do. As I was the only Irish speaker in the area, they came to me. Basically paid for my uni.

I used to be a street sweeper. You might think cleaning up at 4am on a Sat and Sun morning is a shit job, but the amount of free stuff I found made up for it. Cash, drugs, clothes. In one year, I found and sold six phones.

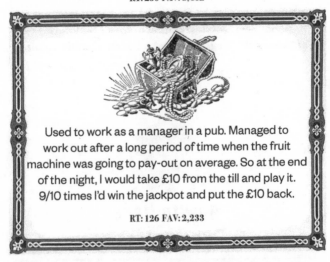

Used to work as a manager in a pub. Managed to work out after a long period of time when the fruit machine was going to pay-out on average. So at the end of the night, I would take £10 from the till and play it. 9/10 times I'd win the jackpot and put the £10 back.

While working at a college, one of my colleagues started selling worn tights on a fetish website to make ends meet. Her orders got so large that half the staff in the A-level department were helping her out by wearing a pair each most days. Only 2 of the 8 staff were women.

Money-Saving Tips

~~~~~~

Britain's top money-saving expert MARTIN LOOPISS on how to survive the credit crunch.

~~~~

I recently emigrated and left all my stuff behind. The walls of my new place are bare and I don't have much money for art. When I see a cute, well-photographed dog on Twitter, I take a screenshot and put it in an A5 frame. My walls are filling up nicely with pics of all your pets.

RT: 325 FAV: 15.7K

I bought a house in Spain at a ridiculous price, but I never told my wife it was so cheap because the last owner murdered his wife and children and hanged himself in it, and none of the locals would touch it with a ten-foot pole. We're moving there in a month.

RT: 356 FAV: 3,695

I always book Any Time Return train tickets with work. When I get home, I check to see if any trains were significantly delayed on my route, then claim I was on that service and get the refund paid directly to myself.

RT: 210 FAV: 5,371

I used to squirt shampoo into my hand at Tesco on the walk back from uni, then walk home and straight into the shower with it clasped there, to save having to waste money on it.

RT: 272 FAV: 4,341

My husband likes orange juice from the milkman but it's extortionate, so on milkman days I fill up an empty milk bottle with Asda orange juice.

RT: 75 FAV: 2,416

I bought a flat that had an electricity meter.
I had no idea who the electricity was with, so I kept putting
a pound in the meter. Eventually it was full, so I broke it open
and just started using the same pound coin over and over.
That was 15 years ago & it's still working today.

**I don't buy shower gel. I check the recycling bin at the
gym – blokes often discard bottles when there's only a
bit left. That bit left can do 10–20 more showers. I like
to think I'm doing my bit for the planet as well as my
pocket. Plus I smell different each month.**

Whenever I go into Currys or PC World, I set all the PCs
and tablets to my company website. Had loads of good
feedback, new customers and not a single complaint.
Fuck paid advertising.

Ideas for Projects
to Rival Fesshole

~~~~~~

*Stuck for a project to suck up your hours when you're not
working or sleeping? Why not get a hobby?*

~~~~

I set up a complaint box at work. People think HR set it up, but
it was me. At the end of every week, I take the box home and
read about all this petty drama that's built up.

Little-known fact, but it costs only £1.50 to get a copy of the will of anyone who's died in the last 25 years from the gov.uk website. Whenever I'm bored, I search for a dead celebrity's will and have a poke around their business like a nosy bastard.

I once filled an entire C90 cassette with recordings of my farts. I wish I still had it. I would say it's my life's greatest achievement. I'm a partner in a firm of solicitors and I'm 63.

I keep a spreadsheet of famous people who have two first names – e.g. George Michael, Paula Abdul, etc. – I don't know why I do this, but there are currently 514 names on it.

If I'm bored, I use dating apps just to find someone to go out for a drink with and I don't see it as a date. There should be an app for people wanting to go out.

Advice

**I have a spreadsheet where I rank milk based on
how well the plastic top peels off. Aldi currently on top:
zero foil remains, great peel.**

RT: 295 FAV: 5,838

I'm a bit embarrassed to admit I have an interest in air-raid
sirens. I've installed a live map to go around hunting them
down and listening to them when they're being tested
annually. I get such an adrenaline rush! I'm a 27-year-old
woman and I feel I should be 60.

RT: 571 FAV: 3,069

**I'm 26 and can't wait to retire. I have made a
countdown calendar but have over 40 years left on it.
This depresses me every time I think about it.**

RT: 324 FAV: 2,684

The Joy of Playing Minor Pranks

*Some inspiring ideas for you to play pranks in your life – although
be careful here, it might make you into a bit of a knobend.*

~~~~

I'm Chinese and love to ask people why they have 'butthole'
tattooed on themselves. I can't even read Mandarin.

RT: 140 FAV: 1,475

**Went on a house viewing. Ridiculously overpriced & stank
of wet dogs. There was a huge, work-in-progress jigsaw
puzzle covering the whole dining table – only the outline
complete, with a mountain of pieces. I couldn't resist
taking one of the pieces on my way out for time wasted.**

RT: 135 FAV: 3,736

For a year, I have been pranking my best mate. I got hold of about 500 keys and tags, and put his name and number on them all. I drop a few sets on the floor, leave them on buses, trains or in coat pockets when I'm looking through clothes at a store. He's slowly going mad.

Whenever I need to transfer money into someone else's account, I always name the transaction 'BIG RON'S DILDOS'...

I once saw a detectorist working on St Ives beach. Delighted to offer him endless hours of entertainment by planting a collection of bottle tops just as the tide was coming in. Next day I poured myself a beer and watched the consequences from my harbour-view flat.

I tell people I don't believe in otters, and that they are just wet cats. Has become legend. Went to a zoo once; was dragged to the otter mound to have their existence proven. No otters. Vindicated.

Advice

Friend wanted to try LSD, so we cut a tiny square from a comic and gave it to her. She spent the next 24 hours 'tripping' thinking she was a frog.

RT: 108 FAV: 3,182

Stag party. We discover the stag's iPhone PIN is 1234. We log in to his Moonpig app and send him a *Frozen*-themed photo card with his mate's nut sack on. His wife and young daughter open the card at home. Sorry.

RT: 86 FAV: 2,376

Aged 14, my friends and I were photographed in the local rag turning our backs on Prince Andrew, who was opening a new building in town. The paper was full of letters complaining about the disrespectful youth of today. I think that we were genuinely ahead of the curve.

RT: 241 FAV: 6,384

The Joy of Trolling Strangers

~~~~~~

Is there a greater joy than slightly winding up strangers?
Yes, there is, there's drugs and sex.
Still, if you're bored of those two, it's a close third.

~~~~

My favourite thing to do at gigs is to sing really loudly but badly so that people who film all the songs have their videos ruined.

RT: 357 FAV: 6,238

I like to sound my car horn at complete strangers whenever I travel to a new town. I then proceed to wave enthusiastically at them to make sure they spend the rest of the day wonderingwhy the guy in the Audi was waving at them. Drives the wife mad.

RT: 273 FAV: 3,210

In the supermarket, I will loudly say things like, 'Without DNA they can't prove anything,' to my wife as we walk past people. The looks are priceless – give it a try sometime.

RT: 414 FAV: 7,861

Sometimes in public I'll loudly pretend I'm engaged in a business deal on my phone. 'I'll take four point eight million. I'm not going any lower than that.' I know it's sad.

RT: 129 FAV: 2,115

When out for a meal, I unscrew the top of the salt shaker and leave it loose on the top before I leave. I never get to experience the carnage this causes as the next patrons to use it try to season their meals, but it hasn't stopped me and my 15-year reign of condiment-based terror.

RT: 345 FAV: 3,013

I've got my 11-year-old daughter involved in burying every foreign coin we get in change or find on the street etc. in our back garden, in the hope that in a couple of hundred years they are discovered by a very confused archaeologist.

I'm a picture framer. I have a friend who's a particularly obnoxious Man U fan. When he asked me to frame several large prints of his wife and family, I hid photos of Jürgen Klopp inside the frames. It's the little victories.

When I was about 14, I realised that 10p would buy me a three-second phone call to the USSR. I used to go out from school at lunchtime to one of the nearby telephone boxes, call a random number in Moscow, and when someone answered yell, 'KGB! KGB! STALIN!' and put the phone down.

How to Digitally Troll Like a Troll Master

~~~~~~

Information technology is a marvellous thing that allows you to irritate people all over the globe from the comfort of your Amstrad emailer.

~~~~

Me and a friend once posted a Gumtree ad looking for actors to audition for our fictitious play *Frasier: The Musical* just so we could get people to send impressions of the characters.

There's a Wi-Fi-connected printer somewhere near my shop. It's not password protected and I've been sending pictures of big penises to it for ages. Just found out it's the printer in the funeral parlour next door. Sorry.

RT: 553 FAV: 7,150

I got an alert someone else was using my Spotify account, so I kept changing the song they were listening to 'I Cum Blood' by Cannibal Corpse. A few hours later, I realised I hadn't reset the Google home device I'd sold to an old lady.

RT: 382 FAV: 7,968

When I'm bored, I sometimes find collaborative playlists on Spotify with names like 'Praise & Worship' and add the filthiest, sweary songs I can think of to them.

RT: 79 FAV: 3,346

I once wrote a quick BASIC program on a ZX Spectrum in my local Tandy's asking users to enter a three-digit number, and no matter what number you entered, a message appeared saying you'd won the computer.

RT: 215 FAV: 2,421

I join local town/village grumbler Facebook groups with a fake account, despite being nowhere near. I get a kick out of winding up NIMBYs. My favourite is saying I saw a local councillor not pick up dog poo or that they're mates with someone building houses. They lose their fucking minds.

RT: 195 FAV: 2,997

Joined loads of 'Brits Abroad' groups on Facebook and stirred thing up by warning them about baked beans and Cadbury shortages. It is cheaper than watching a fireworks display.

RT: 228 FAV: 5,152

My friend and I once found a girl's phone in a nightclub. It was unlocked, so we texted 'I'm pregnant' to 'Dad' before handing it in to reception.

RT: 69 FAV: 2,535

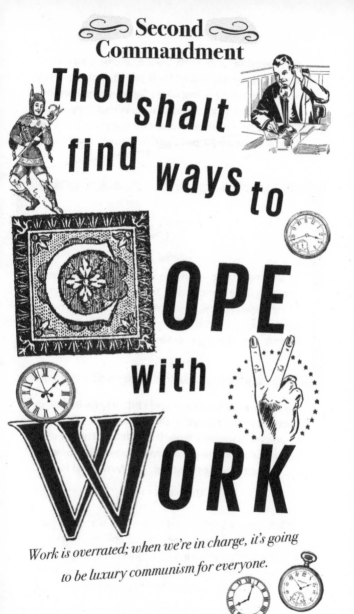

Second Commandment

Thou shalt find ways to COPE with WORK

Work is overrated; when we're in charge, it's going to be luxury communism for everyone.

I used to work with someone who was so catastrophically shit at their job that much of my time was spent fixing basic fuck-ups caused by their laziness and ineptitude. When they left, the office had a whip-round and I pretended to put in some money, but I actually took out £20.

RT: 187 FAV: 4,529

I used the phrase 'wrong end of the brush' in a team meeting the other day and everyone laughed at me. But 'wrong end of the stick' makes no sense. Both ends are the fucking same. Mine makes much more sense. Been stewing about it ever since. Ruined my whole day.

RT: 214 FAV: 1,736

I'm a senior IT engineer and I bitterly ridicule the 'turn it off and on again' thing from *The IT Crowd* whenever someone trots it out. In reality, though, I've made an £80k career mostly by just knowing what to turn off and on, and how to do it.

RT: 273 FAV: 4,773

A lad at work knocked into me while I was carrying several mugs of tea, causing minor spillage. He didn't apologise, just gave me a dismissive look and walked off. This was 8 years and 3 jobs ago, but I will hate him until the heat death of the universe.

RT: 160 FAV: 5,512

During lockdown I was rejected for a £110k job for being 'too serious and professional for the company culture'. I'd done the whole Zoom interview naked from the waist down because I'd spilt Ribena on my lap just before it started. My balls kept sticking to the desk chair.

I once worked with a group of people so awful that I volunteered to be the office First Aider, on the off-chance that if one of them had an accident, I could actively and knowledgeably not provide any assistance.

A colleague constantly talks about his partner of 6 years. The rest of us have never met her so we assume she's made up. Got a group chat going on specifically to track mentions of her, checking for contradictions. We have no idea how to question him about this diplomatically.

I always cut my hair with electric trimmers. Recently, the 12mm attachment fell off mid-stroke, leaving a long skinhead strip over the top of my head. To cover it up, it all came off. I told everyone at work that I did it for charity, raising £217.00.

Work

Just had to deny having a secret office toaster to the building manager while eating a piece of toast. This is the closest I'll ever get to being in an episode of *Seinfeld*.

Three years ago, I wondered what would happen if I stopped reading my work emails. 109,086 unread emails later: 28% salary increase, two bonuses and four restricted stock awards. No one knows I don't read my email.

Master Technology to Make Your Job Easier

The trick with work is to subcontract everything to someone else on the internet. This sentence was written by Barryski in Moscow for 1p.

~~~~

I have been training my children to interrupt tedious Zoom meetings with colleagues to allow me to get on with some actual work. They get £1 a go, and will interrupt upon receiving a WhatsApp.

The new guy in marketing pitched a brand idea to the MD, who loved it. I bought the domain name anonymously for 89p during the meeting on my laptop. They ended up paying me £2,000 for the URL.

Every Friday at 10am, I head to the meeting room I've booked for my weekly '2022 Budget Update' meeting. There is no meeting – I set it up so I can do a Morrisons grocery shop via Amazon undisturbed.

RT: 151 FAV: 6,048

If you leave your desk for an hour, people question where you are. If you leave your desk for an hour and take your laptop and a notepad, no questions are asked. I've been taking my laptop and notepad to the toilet and having some 'me time' at least three times a week.

RT: 53 FAV: 2,402

I often sit and work at my laptop wearing headphones. People think I'm listening to music. Am I fuck. I just don't want to talk to you.

RT: 580 FAV: 106

I automated about 80% of my previous job with some easy Excel scripts and obscure Chrome plug-ins. Nobody knew about it and they thought I just worked really hard. I even scheduled my emails throughout the day to make it appear like I was working.

RT: 66 FAV: 2,658

Work

I always send emails a couple of minutes before I leave work so I don't have to deal with the replies until the next day, or ideally until after the weekend.

Every Wednesday afternoon, I would put a 2-hour meeting for CCS on my Outlook calendar. The senior managers would always ask, 'How's CCS getting on?' I would reply, 'Brilliant, they love our attendance and we are forging a great relationship.' CCS is Costa coffee shop.

I used to work in a call centre. I'd look at the call-waiting screen, and when I was next in line to take a call, I'd call the call centre from my internal phone, pretend I couldn't hear the person on the other end and hang up. I'd move to the back of the queue. My stats were insane.

I've been promoted twice since 2020 despite averaging 4–5 hours of Football Manager each day. I delegate boring tasks to my team and share them with my bosses as huge successes. I even watch fake YouTube vids of conference calls to make my Mrs think I'm in meetings.

The publisher of the video game I was working on threatened to pull funding if the game didn't maintain a steady 30 frames per second. It ran at 20 at best. We couldn't optimise it any more, so eventually just wrote some code that added 10 to the FPS counter. They were happy, game shipped on time.

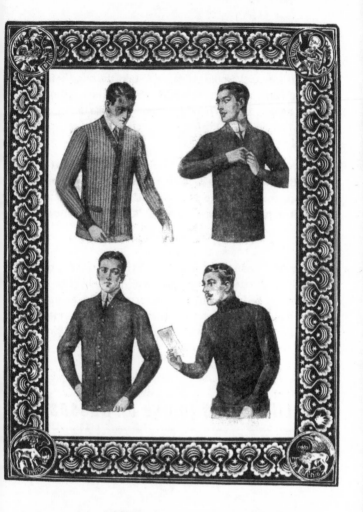

I always join MS Teams meetings slightly late
to avoid small talk with colleagues.

I used to sit in an office with a printer shared with other offices. Someone from down the corridor who was a massive prick would print to it. I'd take the page before he'd arrive to get it. He'd strop off and send it again & again & again. Then I'd put the whole pile back in.

My boss was fired for some underhand dealings at work. With him out of the picture, I faked a chain of emails giving me a sizeable pay rise and then enquired with HR on payday as to why my salary hadn't gone up.

I am a 50-year-old male who works in IT. I regularly post questions to tech forums using a 20-something female persona, as I get better-quality responses. It's amazing how many older male forum-users inbox me with indecent proposals. Stop it chaps, Kitty is not that kinda girl.

Life Hacks to Use on Bosses

~~~~~~

The central message of this book is that you should destroy capitalism from within – and remember, it's the bosses and landlords who'll get hanged first in any revolution.

~~~~

My job is quite niche and my employer didn't increase my pay for around 2 years. So I paid for adverts on job websites for my exact role advertising 1.5x my salary and sent the links to my boss. Got me my desired raise, plus some extra.

I told my manager I'm an alcoholic. I'm not, but I wanted to stop being invited to work drinks with my seriously boring colleagues. It worked.

My boss was pissing me off so I downloaded their CV from LinkedIn and sent it to a ton of recruiters. That boss left within the week.

We had a boss who was pure evil. It was thought because she wasn't getting any. One person had a mate who said he would sort this for a price. The entire office threw in £5 each. Deed got done. She was nice as pie for a few weeks.

I anonymously sent screenshots of my manager's racist Facebook posts to HR. A few days later we were told my manager had left the company. I applied for his role and got it, along with a £15k pay rise.

I know my bosses at work monitor our internet access and there is a massive shortage of engineers in my field. So once every few months, I've spent a couple of lunchtimes a week googling for job vacancies. Without asking for it, I've just been offered a 30% pay rise.

Strategies to Cope With a Terrible Job

~~~~~~

If you have to work, take inspiration from these people who've found wonderful ways to improve their working lives for the benefit of humanity.

~~~~

A bloke I work with has terrible breath, so I always offer him a Polo mint. However, it would be rude not to offer one to my 6 colleagues I sit with also... I end up going through a pack of Polos a day and must have spent at least £100 on bloody Polos just because of some troglodyte.

In the Morrisons annual staff survey, in the 'How can we be better?' free-text section, I always mentioned, 'We should go back to everyone wearing hats.' I did this for 4 years because it really wound up the idiot who ran the survey. 'Why the hats comments again?' he would fume.

I couldn't stand a guy I used to work with. Every morning he'd make his porridge in the staff microwave. While it was cooking, he'd pop to the loo, so I would give it an extra minute cooking time. It always bubbled over, so he'd have to clean the microwave. Entertained me for two weeks.

I have a folder on my desktop of reports written by a man in a rival company who is awful at his job. Whenever I get imposter syndrome and panic that I don't know what I'm doing, I open them and read through and feel better about myself.

I used to work in a family restaurant and often dressed up as the mascot. I found that if I slid down the plastic slide, it charged up the nylon suit and made me into a walking ball of static energy. So, when the kids used to hug me, I'd electrocute the little bastards.

I am a teacher. I love wearing masks. It allows me to mouth profanities at students that annoy me without them knowing.

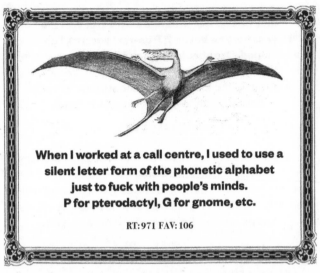

**When I worked at a call centre, I used to use a
silent letter form of the phonetic alphabet
just to fuck with people's minds.
P for pterodactyl, G for gnome, etc.**

RT: 971 FAV: 106

As a recording studio engineer, I've lost count of how many
times bands/producers have asked for more of whatever on
their track. I just turn a knob that does absolutely nothing until
they say, 'That sounds perfect.' Twats.

RT: 761 FAV: 6,999

**I run a web design company. We have a 'cunt tax' for
clients who have been rude to developers or staff, or who
make ridiculous demands. Sometimes this can triple
their bill, just because they were an arsehole.
No client has ever queried the costs.**

RT: 559 FAV: 4,474

I wrote offensive graffiti about myself in the toilets at work,
just so HR had to start an investigation. The level of suspicion
it has caused between my colleagues is so empowering that
I might step up the hate campaign against myself.

RT: 210 FAV: 1,039

I received an 'official warning' from HR for constantly smelling of alcohol while at work. So I cunningly started drinking small bottles of allegedly odour-free vodka instead of my usual cans of lager. That went quite well until I shat myself during our annual board meeting.

While stacking and dressing shelves at a supermarket I work in, I make sure that the products that I really enjoy myself are the best presented as a thanks for high-quality, tasty goods. The Yorkshire Tea bit is always immaculate on my watch. Immaculate. Tetley looks shit.

I was told to make someone redundant by a weak boss who couldn't face it. She came into the meeting, started crying and told me she was resigning as she couldn't bear working for the boss. I told her to keep quiet, shredded her letter and told her to take the £12,000 payout.

Petty Revenge at Work

~~~~~~

Fucking with colleagues and clients is pretty much the only reason to work. Well, there's money, of course, but does money truly bring the same joy as outright malice?

~~~~

I was photographing a wedding and a female guest was exceptionally rude to myself and everybody else there, so while editing, I made her teeth banana-yellow in every picture.

My MD has increased all fees he charges to clients because of increased energy bills and costs etc. But he hasn't increased our salaries because he 'can't afford it', so we always leave the lights on overnight when we leave for the day. He fucks off at 2pm most days, so has no idea.

RT: 121 FAV: 7,496

I was made redundant about 18 months ago. I understand times were hard during the pandemic, but it was blunt and sneaky. I logged into the company Dropbox account and permanently deleted a load of files as I knew they never backed up.

RT: 54 FAV: 2,217

I used to own my own business and during consultation with customers used to ask if they liked football. I would ask which team they followed, and if the reply was Man Utd, I would joke that the price had just gone up 10%. We would all laugh, but I would actually add 10%.

RT: 601 FAV: 103

There was a new guy in my office that really got on my nerves. One day he asked me to set an out of office for him, so I wrote: 'Thank you for your email, I'm currently on anal leave,' knowing he was useless and would never check it.

RT: 117 FAV: 3,270

I'm an accountant. Every Christmas we have a vote for the client who's been the biggest prick of the year, then I report them to HMRC, regardless of whether they have done anything wrong. Invariably they get a full audit, and we get more work: it's a win-win.

RT: 198 FAV: 2,625

Terry the consultant once called me 'just an administrator'. For the next 12 months, his internet connection kept failing; just his, no one else in the company. He'd have to call me, but neither he nor this administrator could figure out how it kept randomly happening. Sorry Terry.

RT: 106 FAV: 3,207

As a taxi driver, I took a scrote into town. On arrival, he said he had no money & monkey-walked off, all cocky, laughing. I drove back to his house & squeezed super glue into his door lock. Next day I drove past & saw a joiner replacing a smashed-in front door.

RT: 291 FAV: 6,026

I once worked in a mind-numbing office and decided to put a colleague's lease car for sale in the local ads at a bargain price. He received over 90 calls and I could hear him going nuts across the office. Especially as the contact name was Timmy, and he hated being called that.

RT: 131 FAV: 2,916

I made coffee for my workmate twice a day and each week I upped the amount of coffee by half a teaspoon. He was on 13 teaspoons of coffee per cup when I finally told him.

RT: 33 FAV: 538

Ten years ago, I was made redundant from the magazine I worked for. Every time I've seen it on sale since, I've hidden it behind copies of other mags. I will do this until the day I die.

RT: 115 FAV: 5,346

You Are a Secret Agent Undermining Productivity From Within

If we work together, we can lower productivity to the levels of the 1970s and pop music will get good again.

~~~~

My organisation decided that the statement at the end of all email signatures should also be in Welsh to be inclusive. As the only Welsh speaker, I translated it and added the words 'Here be dragons' at the end. The whole organisation has had this on emails for four years now.

RT: 1,932 FAV: 24K

I'm a very bored professional artist, who like so many others has had to compromise what I want to paint to make sales to pretentious second-home owners. All my paintings have a cock hidden in them, like *Where's Wally*.

RT: 205 FAV: 2,770

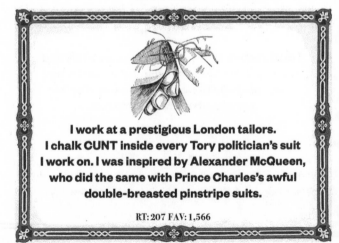

**I work at a prestigious London tailors.
I chalk CUNT inside every Tory politician's suit
I work on. I was inspired by Alexander McQueen,
who did the same with Prince Charles's awful
double-breasted pinstripe suits.**

RT: 207 FAV: 1,566

As the office manager of an advertising agency full of absolute knobs, I secretly switched the coffee supply to decaf for over a year. The smugness of knowing how much shit they used to spout about the power of an espresso was the only thing that got me through the day. Wankers.

I work for a government department. I often submit FOI requests using an anonymous website in the hope that someone will pick up on a story about how corrupt this government is.

Leaving my job soon. There's currently 170 holiday requests put in by staff. We can't afford to get them all covered and we don't have the manpower. There's no audit trail, so the day I leave, I'm approving every single one.

Life Hacks to Make Your Office Very Slightly Better

Work is terrible. But wait, maybe it could be slightly better with some handy-tip-orientated confessions?

~~~~

Every leap year, I take an unjustified sick day. They're not getting an extra day's work out of me for no extra money.

I've recently joined a new company, where everybody else is a heavy drinker. I stopped drinking years ago, so this means I get very quiet mornings to myself while everybody else recovers, and my lack of productivity doesn't stand out. Win-win.

I tell people I work with that my wife doesn't like me going out after work. She's actually cool with it; I just despise my colleagues and don't wish to spend any time with them outside work. It's a cover-all excuse to not do anything with them.

All my grandparents are dead, but I always start new jobs with all 4 alive and well. I make sure to refer to them when chatting to my colleagues. When I need a day or two off, there is a fictional fatality. Works every time. Hardest part is remembering who you've killed off.

I am advertising a job at the moment. I've stipulated 'must be vaccinated'. This isn't coming from a health perspective, it just feels like an effective way of deterring nutters and weirdos.

I accidentally got fanny hair removal cream
in my hair and ended up with a bald patch.
I told people at work I had stress-related
alopecia and would be wearing a hat until my
hair had grown back. They all clubbed together
and bought me a spa day to help me relax.

Work

I went from a £9 per hour data-entry job to a £46,000 per year role initially, simply by copying someone else's CV and reading about their market/industry every night for 2 weeks before my interview to make it sound like I had a clue. Been in the role for 10 years today.

I have started a new job which has a 4-day week. I have told no-one that I am only working Monday to Thursday now, including my partner, who I live with. Fridays are my secret 'me' days free of social obligations.

I once had a manager who would steal all of my creative ideas, so before a big meeting with the directors, I mentioned an idea that was completely against the safeguarding rules of the charity. She pitched it, the CEO went ballistic and she got a disciplinary.

While working at the Co-op, I used to hide a few of the very best Easter eggs behind the toilet roll – then dig them out after Easter, when I could get them for pennies at a discount.

I worked at an Indian takeaway. Sometimes, not long before my shift ended, I'd order a delivery to an address I knew was vacant. When it was returned undelivered, the boss would give it to me rather than throw it away.

Insider Info Gleaned From People Who Have Jobs. Remember Jobs?

~~~~~~

Do you want some 'facts' about how the world really works? We're here to help.

~~~~

Everybody gets caught up in the mysticism and secrets of Freemasonry. I joined a lodge about seven years ago, so I'll let you in on one of the secrets. It's fucking boring as fuck.

RT: 273 FAV: 5,481

A few years ago, I moved to China on business. The job fell through but I had already paid rent, so I applied for a job as a 'copywriter'. Turns out it was writing fake online reviews. They had 1000s of employees and worked for many well-known brands. Don't trust ANYTHING online.

RT: 352 FAV: 51,737

The film *Hot Fuzz* is the most accurate portrayal of policing I have ever seen. I was a copper for 30 years in the deepest West Country, and the film was frighteningly realistic.

RT: 384 FAV: 5,063

**Worked for a Cabinet MP. The idea that there's
an orchestrated global campaign to oppress us is
laughable. He genuinely cares more about the RSPB and
wheelie bins than anything else. Oh, and getting
re-elected, of course.**

I am a sommelier at a top restaurant in London. I can't tell
the difference between any of the wines, and when asked
about them I just read the description on the website we
buy them from.

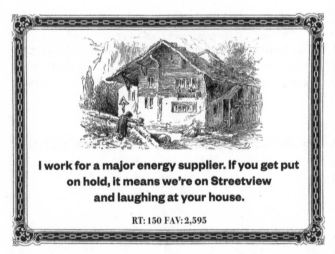

**I work for a major energy supplier. If you get put
on hold, it means we're on Streetview
and laughing at your house.**

I work in the IT department. I can see everyone's Google
searches. My faves include: 'Are children with autism
smaller', 'Controversial and contentious women', 'Can you
outrun a horse', 'Why would an engaged person cheat'.
And from the CEO: 'Kate Middleton topless'

You Fucked Up at Work So Bad

~~~~~~

Take courage from these fine people who have fucked up more than you have – you'll be fine.

~~~~

I'm a PT. Took on a very large client who was very nervous about sitting on her new exercise ball. I reassured her: 'You'd have to be the size of an elephant to pop it, don't worry!' She confidently sat down, but the moment her arse sunk into the ball, it exploded. Mortifying.

RT: 271 FAV: 12.4K

I had a job to get unemployed folk back to work. My first success was a bloke that I got a job as porter at the local hospital. He was arrested & in the papers 6 months later. He'd been caught having sex with dead bodies & I'd used him as my case study for our laminated brochure.

RT: 445 FAV: 9,253

Working on an old piano in a pub. It was filthy inside, so I vacuumed up what I thought was an extraordinary amount of fag ash. Turned out the pub's regular pianist had died recently, and as a tribute to him the landlord had tipped his ashes inside...

RT: 176 FAV: 4,313

I'm a jeweller and once had a locket to repair that contained a loved one's lock of hair, which I carefully removed. The repair was delicate and I held my breath while doing it. As I finished, I let that breath go and it blew the hair away. The locket now contains some of my hair.

RT: 138 FAV: 3,404

Life Tip - Don't Be a Twat
to Anyone Serving You

*Just be nice, OK? It's not hard, and also there's a thing called
'enlightened self-interest' where if you're nice,
people will be nicer back.*

~~~~

**I work as a waiter. If anyone is on a date and trying to
impress a girl and is even slightly rude to me, I wait
until they have taken a big bite of food before asking if
everything is OK with their food. It soothes me.**

RT: 157 FAV: 5,743

When I worked in retail – the worst years of my life –
I kept a tiny magnet at the cash register.
If a customer was a jerk, I would de-magnetize
their bank cards. I did it a lot.

RT: 96 FAV: 3,212

**I work for a bank call centre. I absolutely try to make
your life harder if you yell at me for things I can't control.**

RT: 105 FAV: 2,985

Working in a call centre in 2005, my colleagues & I would keep details of customers who were rude to us. We'd call their homes from pay phones on our way back from nightclubs, asking them, by name, to discuss their anger issues with us. If anything, it just made them more angry.

I work in a call centre for a major company. If I take a dislike to the way a customer is speaking to me, I will simply cut them off. But I do it mid-sentence so it sounds like an accident/technical glitch. I take extra pleasure from this when wait times are 30 minutes plus.

I'm a paramedic and got called to a complete cunt. He was a real piece of work, demanding this and that with nothing actually wrong with him. As we walked outside to go to hospital as he had demanded, I switched off his freezer. Bastard.

When I worked in a call centre, some entitled arsehole gave me a mouthful on the phone. I jotted down his email address and signed him up to every pornography pop-up I came across for a month. Being 19 at the time, you can imagine how many that was.

I once worked for a major broadband supplier. If I had a particularly nasty customer on the line, I would keep his set-top box details. When I could see they were watching England play, I would reboot the box, just when they were about to score. I had a huge list of people.

Teachers Are Excellent

All teachers are excellent. Imagine having to put up with arsehole kids all day. You people are HEROES.

~~~~

As a postgrad, earned a bit of cash supervising undergraduate exams. Relieved the boredom playing Battleships against the other supervisor. Stand behind a student to fire a shot. Opponent gives silent nod or headshake for hit or miss.

RT: 139 FAV: 2,437

I'm an Early Years teacher. One of many small victories of my job is being able to trump in class and nobody thinks it's you. I've been blaming 4-year-olds for farts, with the standard cover-up line 'Does somebody need the toilet?', since 2009.

RT: 169 FAV: 4,465

As a young teacher I realised that a wordsearch kept a difficult class quiet and busy for the last 10 minutes of a lesson, especially if a bag of sweets was on offer for the first to finish. I always left one word out so they could never finish.

RT: 1,010 FAV: 3,612

I'm a teacher. My 'World's Best Teacher' staffroom mug;
I bought it for myself.

**I'm a primary school teacher. 99% of the time,
if you're a dick, your child will be a dick too.
Parents night always confirms this. We mock
you as we compare stories in the staffroom.**

Working at a girls' school, we all dressed up for World
Book Day. I chose to be Mark Renton from *Trainspotting*.
Halfway through the day, I froze in panic as I realised
I'd dressed as a character who shags a schoolgirl.

**Just had a verbal warning for saying a lad's
haircut makes him look like Princess Diana.
It's shit being a teacher.**

Two kids scratched their names into a desk in my classroom.
After the class had left, I got a compass and scrawled 'suck
each other's cocks' underneath.

Why Transport Workers Are the Best People in the World

~~~~~~

The comedy genius of bus and train drivers – who knew?

~~~~

I'm a bus driver. I allow everyone to travel, no matter what: fake pass, out of date, I don't care. Every time someone does it, I say to myself, 'Fuck you, First Bus!'

RT: 226 FAV: 1,913

I'm a train driver and every time I go past a golf course, if someone is about to tee off or play a shot, I give a nice toot of my horn to test their concentration levels.

RT: 523 FAV: 13.3K

I drive trains for a living. At some stations there are spots on the platform so people know where the doors will be when we stop. When I'm bored, I deliberately creep along the platform and stop a few metres out of place, just to watch commuters sidle up the platform like crabs.

RT: 414 FAV: 7,396

As a bus driver, I like to play a game called 'pass or pensioner'. When an OAP scans their bus pass, the expiry date comes up on the ticket machine screen. I like to decide which I think will expire first, the pass or the pensioner.

RT: 408 FAV: 8,070

My teacher always told me, 'You won't get a job staring out the window all day.' I work as a tube driver now on £68k a year and literally stare out the window all day.

RT: 656 FAV: 16K

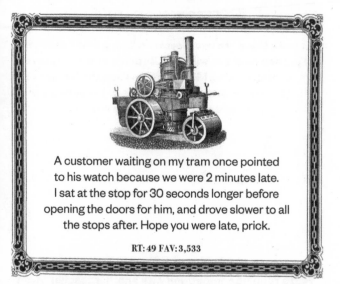

A customer waiting on my tram once pointed
to his watch because we were 2 minutes late.
I sat at the stop for 30 seconds longer before
opening the doors for him, and drove slower to all
the stops after. Hope you were late, prick.

RT: 49 FAV: 3,533

I'm a train driver. When we see staff working on the tracks, we are trained to blast our horn at them and they have to raise their hand to acknowledge. Whenever this occurs, I shout in the cabin, 'Put your hands up if your missus doesn't suck your dick.' It's my daily treat.

RT: 153 FAV: 3,365

I'm a bus driver. If I'm having a bad day at work, I'll look in the
mirror while driving and mutter to myself, 'You're all cunts
aren't you?' and then tap the brakes twice so they all nod.

RT: 5,219 FAV: 56.4K

Impromptu Games We Play at Work

~~~~~~

*Anything to alleviate the tedium of late-stage capitalism –
oh climate change, come end it all.*

~~~~

**At work there are two elevators. Every time I use them,
I guess which one will open its doors and keep score.
I'm currently losing 143–89. When I'm right, it makes me
feel better for getting it right but sad because it's the
highlight of my day. I want a new job.**

RT: 34 FAV: 2,434

I have a secret reward system for myself at work.
When I manage to behave in a way I like, I move a paper clip
from 1 pot into another. It's simple, but watching them
increase is a motivator & when I feel tension rising,
I breathe & think, 'Try and get a paper clip'.

RT: 197 FAV: 5,405

**Had a running competition with another teacher to get
Britpop song lyrics into school assembly messages.
Lost when he raised his mic Gallagher-style while
wearing a parka and shades for the Lord's Prayer.
He's a Catholic school headteacher now.**

RT: 123 FAV: 3,517

I've spent the last 6 months on video conference calls
tapping SOS for 1 minute with my index finger on my
shoulder. It's safe to say that this test was a failure.
If I was ever held hostage and needed to let someone
know that I'm in danger, I'm a dead man.

RT: 145 FAV: 2,824

Every morning since 1st January this year, I have been throwing a teabag into my cup from a distance of about 2 metres. It's not that far, but I haven't missed yet. Every morning, the pressure builds as I try to make it a calendar year without missing. It's getting very tense.

How to Make Your Commute Easier

~~~~~~

Commuting is a capitalist con, in that you have to pay to get to the office and you don't even get paid for the time it takes. Plus it's hard to play Nokia Snake while driving.

~~~~

When the Trainline app asks me 'Is the train busy?', I always answer yes, to deter upcoming travellers from ruining my enjoyment of an empty carriage.

I reserve a seat on the train and sit in the unreserved seat next to it. Always have space to relax.

Prior to Covid, I used to travel on trains a lot. I loved a table to myself, enabling me to work. To get a table to myself, I would carry a four-pack of Stella. Arrive on train, place four-pack on table and pretend to fall asleep. As soon as train started, Stella put away and laptop out.

I never used to buy an umbrella. As an ex-commuter, I just used to contact the lost property at Liverpool St and say I'd left a black umbrella on a train a few days ago. They're more common than pigeon shit on a statue, so there were always plenty to choose from. Dump and repeat.

RT: 92 FAV: 2,098

The Joy of Playing Minor Pranks at Work

~~~~~~

Possibly at risk at being a bit of a Colin Hunt if you take this section too literally. BTW: The best trick to play on your colleagues is to advertise their job on monster.co.uk.

~~~~

I spent the entire shift of a dull student job listening to two female colleagues chatting in Greek, punctuated by filthy laughs. When I got up to go, I gave them a cheery smile and said *kalinikta* – good night. The panic on their faces was priceless. It's the only Greek I know.

RT: 177 FAV: 12K

When people leave work and their leaving card is doing the rounds, I write hearts and kisses under other people's names, the more inappropriate the better.

RT: 370 FAV: 11K

Had a mug printed with a colleague's face on it for his birthday. When he's away from his desk, we occasionally use the picture to unlock his shitty phone and order toys for his kids from Amazon.

Each month at work, I turn the crap modern art paintings 90 degrees clockwise. Nobody has ever noticed.

I used to like to take a screen grab of a colleague's desktop, put all their shortcuts in a folder, then use the screen grab pic as their desktop image. Watching them click on inactive icons provided hours of mirth. No, I don't have any friends.

Work colleague is freaked out as I keep joining Teams calls wearing the same or similar outfit and he can't understand why. Thinks our minds are linked. His wife or another member of the team actually tell me in advance so I can change. 18 months and we're still not bored.

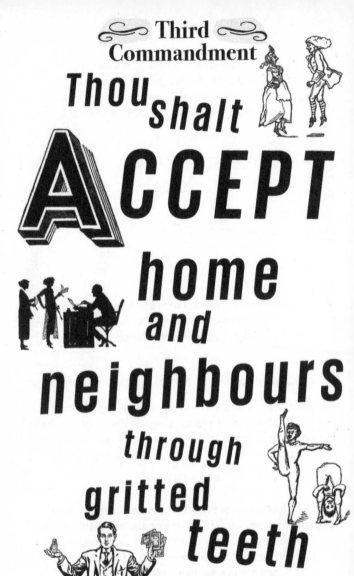

Third Commandment

Thou shalt

ACCEPT

home
and
neighbours
through
gritted
teeth

Ever had a neighbour over for coffee?

Horrible, isn't it? Never do it.

New neighbours kept 'popping by' for a cup of tea. No amount of hints worked. One day they caught me and invited themselves in for a cuppa. When they'd finished, I put their cups on the floor for the dog to clean and popped them back in the cupboard. They never did pop by again.

My braindead neighbour said I am 'irresponsible' for having flowers in my garden as her child might get stung by a bee. I made a new flower bed right next to the fence and also throw seeds over her side whenever she is out. Needless to say, we are not speaking.

We had a Jubilee street party. It was fun but I feel as though we are now expected to chitchat and behave like lifelong friends. I miss the times when you could walk past without speaking to anyone. Is there a way to retrace our steps?

My housemate's bed and mine are separated by a very thin wall. There's no privacy. She wakes up every morning to a lovely, gentle, floaty alarm chime, so I chip in with a big, meaty fart. Proper push it out. I hear a disappointed sigh every time.

I'm a single bloke in my 40s and live next door to a family. They have 3 cute kids. I don't want to be the strange bloke from next door handing out sweets, so I send anonymous Amazon sweet parcels to them a couple of times a year.

Petty Revenge on Neighbours

'Hell is other people, especially that twat at no 11.' Jean-Paul Sartre

Neighbour really pissed me off once, can't remember why. For the next few weeks, I'd get up early on bin day and bring his full bin in and then put it back out once the lorry had gone. He would go fucking ballistic when he found his bin still full.

RT: 406 FAV: 9,754

Years ago, we borrowed a Thermos from family I don't much like. They're gammony and materialistic, but too polite to mention we didn't return it. I make sure it appears in a few FB pics each year on outings, because I know it will irritate the hell out of them if they see it.

RT: 176 FAV: 3,479

There's a Tesla parked overnight at the end of my road. The owner runs a cable out of their front door to charge it. I tripped over it once. Now I unplug it every night when I take the dog out for a piss.

RT: 275 FAV: 7,375

Old prick who lives across the road got in an argument
with my mother, made her cry. Next day I noticed he left
his front door open when he was in back garden.
I entered quickly and stole one shoe from each of the five
pairs neatly lined up in the hall. Still feel great about it.

RT: 130 FAV: 2,619

**There's one guy who lives on the top floor of our block
of flats, and he never sends the lift back to the ground
floor. So whenever I notice him going for a cigarette,
I send the lift to the top floor. Petty, but I love it.**

RT: 133 FAV: 2,333

Stoner in flat upstairs would put on loud music at 1am.
Ignored request to turn it down. Other neighbour showed
me mains switches for flats. Any time music started late,
his power went off until I left for work next day.
Enjoyed hearing him trying all his plugs and lights.

RT: 81 FAV: 5,485

**I hate my neighbour that much that every few weeks, at
night, I move their satellite dish. It fills me with joy when
they have to call the Sky engineer to realign at £50 a time.**

RT: 102 FAV: 2,094

My neighbour fell out with me & would send taxis & pizzas to my house in the early a.m. One night I had enough. The following morning I rang the undertakers pretending to be her partner & that afternoon she opened her door to them coming to collect the body. She stopped.

RT: 325 FAV: 9,211

My neighbour is obsessed with his lawn and once reached over and cut the top off my walnut tree, claiming it was shading his lawn too much. Every couple of weeks, I launch a couple of handfuls of granular weedkiller over the fence.

RT: 96 FAV: 6,413

If my Brexity neighbour spots me when I'm returning from a bike ride, he always asks how far I've gone. I always answer in km because it winds him up.

RT: 457 FAV: 11.5K

Petty Revenge (Housing and Letting Edition)

How do you make people click 'like' on the internet? Post 'All landlords are bastards.'

Rented my house out while I moved abroad for work. Tenants stopped paying after 3 months and it took about a year to evict them. Haven't seen a penny owed. Going through post afterwards, I saw a cheque with a £1k+ rebate from HMRC for one of them. I tore it up and binned it.

RT: 241 FAV: 7,058

The people buying my house were gits, haggling down the price over little things. When I moved out, I took the wheelie bins with me.

RT: 234 FAV: 6,602

The buyers of our house were a nightmare and kept slowing the whole chain down, so I ordered 30 old keys off eBay. On moving day I left them on the counter with all the other spare house keys, just so their first day as homeowners would be wasted trying to find what they unlocked.

RT: 210 FAV: 377

After getting screwed over by a lettings agent at uni, I decided to open a Twitter account for the agency as they didn't already have one. Played it straight for a while and built up some followers, then started tweeting the worst material I could from them.

RT: 173 FAV: 5,412

I hate my nosy parker landlord, so when Storm Eunice hit, I kicked the fence down and let the weather take the rap. Hope it cost £££ to repair.

RT: 85 FAV: 2,372

The couple buying our flat beat us down on price at the last minute when it was too late to pull out. So in return, I cut every single plant in the garden at the very base. They would have a beautiful-looking garden for 2 days before everything died.

RT: 125 FAV: 3,602

The sellers of our house were arseholes. Didn't take final meter readings, argued about the survey and gave us the moving date we pleaded not to have due to work. They didn't change their postal address. Have great glee in returning post to sender, including car tax and finance.

RT: 106 FAV: 2,418

Animals and Why You Love Them

We all love pets. Couldn't eat a whole one, though – not unless it was a rabbit, we suppose.

~~~~

My dog's legs have gone. The last 10 years I've run with him on the field, with him sitting to give me a few seconds' head start; he's destroyed me every time. I barely jog now, but let him feel he's still the man as he gets ahead of me, and he turns, wagging his tail in pride.

RT: 444 FAV: 5,889

I always tell my dog I love him. A friend once told me that was 'a bit gay', and I should stop. I cut all ties with said friend, ghosted that motherfucker the very same day. If my Border collie is reading this, love you mate!

RT: 301 FAV: 5,166

I regale colleagues with stories of my 3-year old, Ben. And I occasionally have to leave early because of him. I haven't told them that Ben is my cat.

RT: 290 FAV: 9,180

If the cat is asleep, I won't vacuum until he's woken up. I don't extend the same courtesy to my husband or kids.

RT: 265 FAV: 77,197

When my cat was a kitten, he picked a fight with a crow. Big mistake. Now crows stalk him everywhere. This should really be his confession.

RT: 134 FAV: 2,524

People think it's really weird, but me and my dog share ice cream. My girlfriend thinks it's disgusting that I let the dog lick it and then I continue licking it, but he's such a good boy and I don't think there is anything wrong with his beautiful little tongue.

RT: 408 FAV: 2,482

Our dog has been staying with a friend while we've had Covid. When they dropped her back I thought it'd be like one of those videos where marines come home from a tour and their dog goes mad and everyone cries, but I just got a quick wag and a lie down. I was really hurt.

RT: 94 FAV: 3,542

Since having a water meter fitted, I've tried to flush my toilet as little as possible. I've now become obsessed with this and found myself going outside in the garden with my dog every morning for a dump. It's become a bonding session and my bill is now around £15 a month.

RT: 319 FAV: 2,340

When I dry my dog's paws after he's been in the garden, I pretend I'm the 4th official checking a player's studs. After I'm done I give him a pat on the bum and say, 'Have a good game, son.'

RT: 515 FAV: 8,730

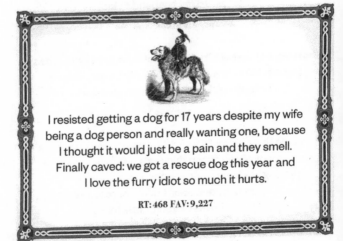

I resisted getting a dog for 17 years despite my wife being a dog person and really wanting one, because I thought it would just be a pain and they smell. Finally caved: we got a rescue dog this year and I love the furry idiot so much it hurts.

RT: 468 FAV: 9,227

I've handed in my notice at my current job. I've given a lot of professional reasons as to why I'm leaving, but the real reason is my new job is home-based and I want to spend my days with the dog instead of the dickheads I currently work with.

RT: 741 FAV: 2,665

Animals and Why Fesshole Readers Shouldn't Be Allowed Near Them

~~~~~~

Some pet owners need to be stopped and reported to the RSPCA.

~~~~

Our dog attacked a hedgehog in the garden. Assumed the hedgehog was dead and put it in the wheelie bin. Next day went to put a bag in there only to find it munching away on some potatoes. Had to dig the poor fucker out from its all-you-can-eat buffet and popped him over the fence.

RT: 417 FAV: 4,486

Was out for a lovely walk on the Scottish coast with my husband. Saw the most beautiful fluffy sheep I've ever seen, jumped over a field wall and ran over to take a photo. The sheep turned and bolted, fell off a cliff and died.

RT: 153 FAV: 4,487

Made the 'cat summoning kissing sound' at my neighbour's cat while it was crossing the road. It stopped and started trotting towards me. Got flattened by a speeding car. Can't ever say anything.

RT: 108 FAV: 2,233

My cat went missing a month ago. He was found and we buried him two weeks ago. Today he came through the window. I'm not sure whose cat I have under my rose bush in the garden, but I'm glad Timothy is back.

RT: 474 FAV: 12

At a Catholic primary school I went to, once in a while we were made to do private confession to a priest. I'll never forget my confession when I was 8 years old was 'I bully my cat'. The priest actually laughed at me.

RT: 227 FAV: 3,239

We got a puppy in lockdown. While furloughed, I taught him to come to me when I make chicken noises. Now it's the only way to call him back if he's running in the park or anywhere else off the lead. My partner hates me for this.

RT: 152 FAV: 4,787

When my dog misbehaves, I whisper into his ear that he is adopted.

RT: 99 FAV: 2,527

After eating, I sometimes wipe my hands on the dog.

RT: 231 FAV: 3,019

I fart into my hand and feed the arse gas to my dog. She loves it. For a really meaty fart, she licks the air to fully appreciate my offering. She's my best friend.

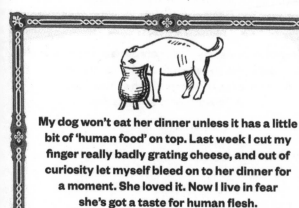

My dog won't eat her dinner unless it has a little bit of 'human food' on top. Last week I cut my finger really badly grating cheese, and out of curiosity let myself bleed on to her dinner for a moment. She loved it. Now I live in fear she's got a taste for human flesh.

Today the cat sat on my desk and left a brown crumb of 'dirt'. I didn't know if it was mud or dry cat poo so I picked it up and sniffed it, and in the process snorted it up into my nostril. Discovered it was shit. I have no one in my life I can tell about this misadventure.

Impromptu Games We Play at Home

~~~~~~

This is the section you should cut out and keep as inspiration for games for you to play when you're so bored you could extract your wisdom teeth just for something to do.

~~~~

**Every Christmas, my mum gets out her address book,
the same one she has used since the 90s.
We have a family competition of 'dead or alive'.
A constantly evolving game.**

When I can't sleep, I play a game where I try and swap sides of the bed with my girlfriend without her waking. I've only managed this twice but I've found a solid tactic in tucking her under the covers and rolling her slowly across the bed. I've named this game 'sausage roll'.

**Sometimes me and my husband shower together
and play a game called 'dick or digit'. It's nothing
sexual, he'll touch my back with either his finger
or his flaccid penis and say 'dick or digit' and
I have to guess which one it is. We both get
really competitive with it.**

My sister and I have a WhatsApp group called 'Foreheads'. We just post photos of people with massive foreheads. No one is safe.

Whenever I can't find anything good to watch on TV, I play a game with myself called 'Put Hitler On'. I almost always find a Hitler documentary at any time of the day or night.

The peak of my boredom during lockdown, which to be honest I'm still an avid fan of in 2022, is Google Street Viewing bakeries in Colombia and seeing which of their pastries I'd most like to try. I have no links to South America and live in Clitheroe, Lancashire, England.

When I get up around 4am, the guy next door is just going to bed. We've got into a routine where every morning he salutes me through his living room window, and I wave back. Not even sure what his name is. My wife thinks it's weird, but it definitely isn't.

Whenever I wake up in middle of the night, I try and 'sense' what the precise time is before checking my phone to see if I am right. This morning I got it spot on: 4.46am. I am really thrilled at my achievement but haven't told anybody as it just sounds weird.

Sometimes when I'm bored, I'll take an egg, go into my garden, and chuck it as far as possible. I usually manage to throw it 6 or 7 gardens down.

I've developed a habit of visiting the Twitter page of porn stars. Not because I want to watch porn, but so I can stalk the profiles of the weird men who reply to every tweet. It's fascinating and awful watching 58-year-old Dave from Barnsley trying to pull some 22-year-old stunner.

Life Hacks for Home

Is your home fucking awful? Here's some handy advice to help. Now you're like that Marie Kondo lady and have thrown your cat in the bin coz it's not sparking joy.

I have a sign on my front door saying: 'Please leave shopping in porch, we have Covid.' We're all Covid-free and it's brilliant at making door-to-door salespeople skip our house and try the next one down.

I keep all the nice cheese behind the tofu in the fridge because I know the greedy shits in this family won't look there. Every night I have a solo cheese fest. Fuck 'em.

RT: 126 FAV: 3,763

I live next door to an unsavoury family. Every day for the last 10 years, when I leave for work I wave goodbye to my wife in the house and shout things like, 'Don't forget to phone your mum.' The truth is I live alone and just don't want the neighbours to burgle my house.

RT: 146 FAV: 3,262

Mother-in-law had become increasingly right-wing. She gets all her news from a Google news feed, so I changed her settings and blocked all of the right-wing newspaper websites and news about the royals. She has become much nicer to be around.

RT: 447 FAV: 8,488

I bought a Ring camera for the front of my house. It has the benefit of seeing parcels while I'm at work, but its best feature is being able to see if the neighbours are outside before I go out or get back so I don't have to engage in small talk. Amazing.

RT: 173 FAV: 4,540

I hated my neighbour's eyesore garden ornament so much I posted an anon Facebook post giving it away. Some random arrived, collected it & drove off. I don't even think the neighbours have noticed yet. Win-win.

RT: 64 FAV: 2,158

HOME & NEIGHBOURS

I spent the whole evening blowing up balloons for the wife's birthday. Felt a bit chesty and out of puff. The following morning, I tested positive for Covid. Two days later, I found my 13-year-old sucking the balloons down like helium. Little fucker wanted 5 days off school.

RT: 162 FAV: 7,350

Some neighbours in my apartment building would leave their shoes out in the corridor. It bothered me a lot, so I put an anonymous notice up in the lobby saying that I'd left my shoes out and somebody took a shit in one of them. Nobody leaves shoes out anymore.

RT: 130 FAV: 3,230

I keep a can of WD-40 in my bathroom. Before every dump I liberally spray the back of the pan, and consequently I haven't left a skidmark in years.

RT: 362 FAV: 3,907

Household Whimsy

~~~~~~

Household whimsy is a defence mechanism against doing chores – you might be able to get out of doing the hoovering if you deliver a few jokes about hoovering to entertain the family. This is how it works, right?

~~~~

Whenever I refill the teabags, if there is only 1 left in the jar, I move it to the top so that it is the next to fulfil its destiny and not consigned to a life of forever being trapped under its teabag friends.

RT: 1,423 FAV: 35.9K

After frying an egg in my mini frying pan, I like to dip the pan
straight into the washing-up bowl so I can pretend I'm
a medieval blacksmith when the water frazzles and spits.

RT: 341 FAV: 7,568

I sing 'Bolognese' to the tune of 'Holiday' by Madonna when I'm cooking one. The lyrics are changeable, based on ingredients used each time.

RT: 152 FAV: 3,754

I convinced my wife that we needed new carpet when we
absolutely didn't. Made sure we bought the fluffiest carpet
available so when I vacuumed I could pretend I was a Premier
League groundsman. The stripes look incredible.

RT: 149 FAV: 7,252

**Every weekend I volunteer to hang out
the washing. We have a spider living in the
peg bag and I'm scared that if the Mrs spots him,
she will make me kill him. We are mates,
I take great care removing/returning pegs
and often apologise for the inconvenience.**

RT: 400 FAV: 9,800

Sometimes when I'm cooking on my gas hob, I pretend I'm a drum and bass DJ and I mix by turning the knobs on my cooker up and down. I'm a mum of two in my late 40s.

RT: 29 FAV: 673

When I'm cooking, if I need to tap the wooden spoon on the saucepan or something, I will without fail think of the start of the BBC cricket theme. I don't even like cricket.

RT: 19 FAV: 346

Sometimes when boiling the kettle, I like to switch it off just before it boils. I like to think that I'm ruining its orgasm.

RT: 138 FAV: 2,096

I have a favourite oven ring. Back right is first choice of the five, regardless of the size of the pan. Front left is my least favourite: definitely the runt of the oven-ring litter.

RT: 365 FAV: 3,593

I like to flick through boxes of After Eight Mints imagining that I'm a giant DJ.

RT: 526 FAV: 4,925

The Joy of Playing Minor Pranks on Neighbours

The best thing to do with neighbours is to fling weedkiller on their plants until they move. Serves them right.

~~~~

If the hippy lady next door is wondering why all her windchimes have been getting gradually higher in pitch over the years, it's because I regularly sneak in to her garden and hacksaw 5mm off the end of one of the pipes.

RT: 434 FAV: 2,126

I was installing a printer for a friend. The next door neighbour's early Wi-Fi printer was unsecured. They were having a huge noisy argument. I transcribed their argument and sent it to their printer. They quickly became quiet.

RT: 164 FAV: 2,479

Remember Secret DJ, the app you could use to choose the music in the venue you were in for free? I realised I could control the jukebox in a Vodka Revolution from my desk in the building next door, so I'd play 'Seven Days' by Craig David on repeat. The staff turned it off after a week.

RT: 127 FAV: 2,983

I used an evening round my neighbour's house to pair my phone with the Bluetooth speaker in their bathroom. Our bathroom is close enough to connect, so when I'm on the loo, I occasionally use the 'Partridge In My Pocket' app to blast out one of Alan's catchphrases. Ah-Ha!

RT: 73 FAV: 1,247

I don't like my neighbour for reasons I won't go into here, so I have set up an old router in my attic which does nothing except broadcast the network name Steve-at-no-6-is-a-cunt to the whole world.

Speaking to Inanimate Objects

'Come on sausages, it's time to cook.'

~~~~

I always say 'thank you' to Alexa so that when AI becomes self-aware and takes over the world, I will be spared enslavement.

I always say 'Hello, slippers' to my slippers, then make them say 'hello' back to me in a silly deep voice. The other day, I unthinkingly added 'I want you in me' and now I feel disgusted.

As a teenager I used to miaow in passing at the family cat, to make him feel included in the conversation. Now I live alone, but I still miaow about the house occasionally, out of habit. My neighbour just asked how my cat is.

Making New Cyber-Pals Online on the Internet Dot Com

~~~~~~

In this age where you can contact almost anyone at any time, many of us are sitting around alone. Reach out to your friend, they need you.

~~~~

When I'm on Zoom, sometimes I mute and smile and say hello to my boyfriend when he's arrived home. I don't have a boyfriend.

RT: 102 FAV: 3,898

My Netflix and Amazon Prime Video accounts were hacked during the first lockdown. Now every time I log on, I get Vietnamese subtitles on whatever I watch. I haven't changed my password as I like the fact I have a connection with someone on the other side of the world.

RT: 44 FAV: 1,937

I work from home and can get lonely, so I've started watching the US *Office* in the background. When people ask how my day has been, I recount the adventures of Dwight as if it's my office but I've changed his name to Dave. Some of my friends feel sorry for Dave.

RT: 38 FAV: 143

I often go into my positive feedback on eBay to cheer myself up. It's lovely seeing that people think I'm a great eBayer and would hope to deal with me again.

RT: 96 FAV: 2,630

Fourth Commandment

Thou shalt

Love

and

Respect

your

ridiculous

family

Can't live with them...

My brother split up with his girlfriend and removed her from the family WhatsApp. But we all really like her, so we created a new group with her, but without him. This has now become the main family WhatsApp.

RT: 1,824 FAV: 3,811

When my little brother was 5, I forged a letter from Woolworths telling him he'd won a Scooby-Doo video. My mum believed it and even took him to collect it. I was shocked when they actually returned with a video. No one ever spoke to me about it. I'm so confused.

RT: 235 FAV: 6,022

Mum's fiancé reacted to me coming out by saying, 'You can't bring some poof to the wedding.' Well the joke's on you, Chris, because it's your son I've been seeing for the last 6 months.

RT: 87 FAV: 2,429

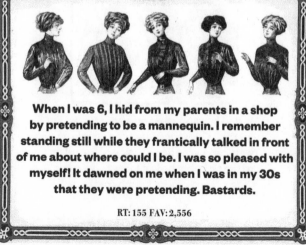

When I was 6, I hid from my parents in a shop by pretending to be a mannequin. I remember standing still while they frantically talked in front of me about where could I be. I was so pleased with myself! It dawned on me when I was in my 30s that they were pretending. Bastards.

RT: 155 FAV: 2,556

My brother-in-law winds me up by constantly telling me how cheap his electric car is to run. Course it's cheap to run, mate, every time you visit us you help yourself to £20+ of our electricity and never bother to offer a penny.

I'm a carer for my mum, who has dementia. This morning I overheard her talking to my dogs. One of them jumped on her lap & she sang 'Melancholy Baby' to him, a lullaby she used to sing to me as a child. I've never cried so hard, yet so quietly.

My dad has appeared on several episodes of BBC *Question Time*. I see people on Twitter accusing him of being a 'Tory plant' all the time, but he just loves politics and is a slightly racist grumpy old man.

My daughter has special needs. Took her
to church at Easter. The vicar loudly
proclaimed 'Hallelujah!' My daughter
immediately shouted 'It's raining men!'
Brought the house down.

Examples of Excellent Parenting That We Could All Learn From

Is your parenting falling into the same old routines? Liven up your 'mum and dad life' by learning from these brilliant parents.

When my son's hamster died I placed it in a carrier bag ready for a burial after school. I later got a phone call from a teacher saying there was a dead hamster in his lunch box. There is also a cheese roll buried in the garden.

RT: 538 FAV: 8,994

At my daughter's 3rd birthday party, I accidentally unplugged the bouncy castle then watched in horror as the screaming toddlers slowly disappeared. 10 years on, one of the kids, now a teenager, is still terrified of bouncy castles.

RT: 53 FAV: 4,087

When my daughter started school we taught her 'Don't accept lifts from strangers, even if they say they're daddy's/mummy's friend who's come to get you.' We put it to the test by sending my mate to pick her up. She replied with, 'Daddy doesn't have friends.' The cheeky shit.

RT: 435 FAV: 164

I put all the paintings and drawings my 5-year-old brings home from school each day in the bin – because they're rubbish. I've done this for the last two years.

RT: 314 FAV: 2,044

When my kids were being potty trained, I told them both that their dad was a champion 'bum-wiperer' and that he'd won medals at big competitions. It basically meant that whenever they went for a poo, they called for him to help them.

I've replaced my daughter's gerbil 3 times and she's not noticed. Last year as part of a school project, she wrote to the _Guinness Book of Records_ to tell them how old it is.

My 4-year-old started entertaining me with pirate noises from her seat in the supermarket trolley. I joined her with lots of 'Arghs' for a good old laugh. I looked around to validate my parenting and feel great, only to see an old man with an eye patch looking very unhappy.

I used to play hide & seek with my toddlers; they'd go upstairs and hide and I'd just sit down with a cuppa and randomly shout out, 'I'm coming!! Where are you?! Oh no, you're not there!' to make them think I was looking for them. Worked a treat for a peaceful 15 mins.

My parents used to make me cross my fingers, make a wish and not speak when I saw a white horse in a field on a car journey. I could speak again when I saw a dog. I was in my 40s before I realised all they were doing was getting a bit of peace and quiet.

Years ago at a toy shop with my 3-year-old son, I hid from him and put on one of those scary *Scream* ghost masks and then jumped out at him. He absolutely freaked out in abject terror and ran away screaming in utter fright. Unfortunately I'd jumped out at someone else's kid.

New Parents Dealing With Babies

~~~~~~

The thing you most need when dealing with new babies is a magic button to allow you uninterrupted sleep.
But we can't offer that, so instead...

~~~~

My wife and I had a baby girl last week, and everybody keeps telling us how beautiful she is... all I see is Ross Kemp. Don't all babies look like one of the Mitchell brothers?

When our baby was 5 months old, I made a deal with my husband. He could do the 11pm feed and the 7am feed and I would do the 2am feed. There was never a 2am feed.

We had twins a year ago. When they were about 3 months old, I gave them both a bath without making sure who was who. My daughter might now actually be her sister.

More Excellent Parents, Dealing With Teens

Honestly, how do you deal with teens as a parent? Impossible – just beg them to not do it on the carpet, though.

I've just told my 16-year-old son that I've received a detailed report of every website he's ever visited from our internet service provider. The look on his face was amazing.

My daughter asked me for help writing a poem about war for her GCSE English. I gave her the lyrics to a song called 'Battle of the Beanfield' by The Levellers. She got an A star.

My son enjoys an occasional doob, so I wait till he's slightly baked to nag him about stuff. I can say, 'Whoever is trimming their pubes over the toilet needs to clean up after themselves' and he just giggles and goes and does it without getting embarrassed. I'm an amazing parent.

Kids Are Shits

~~~~~~

Kids being shits and people thinking kids are shit.
Remember, shitty kids are the shitty adults of tomorrow,
so trip the little fuckers up.

~~~~

**My 2-year-old regularly bursts in while I'm taking a
piss and always asks, 'Daddy, why are you weeing
through your finger?' Thanks, mate, for reiterating
how small my cock is every other day.**

RT: 139 FAV: 3,770

Not mine but my daughter's. When she was about 12
she'd fallen out with a family who lived in the village, so
she made a Sims family of them. She half-starved them,
then built a swimming pool with no ladder, put them all in
and they all drowned. I'm sorry to say I laughed.

RT: 56 FAV: 3,765

**When I was kid doing puzzles with friends, I would
always hide a puzzle piece. At 99.9% completion,
when mass panic ensued, I would always be the
one to heroically find the final piece and complete
the puzzle. I'm 38 now and have no friends.**

RT: 105 FAV: 3,962

In year 9 History, the girl who sat next to me knew I fancied
her, so she copied all my work, which pissed me off. On the
end of year exam I wrote a paragraph about how the French
trained monkey snipers in WWII and this is where 'gorilla
warfare' comes from. I passed, she didn't.

RT: 231 FAV: 5,587

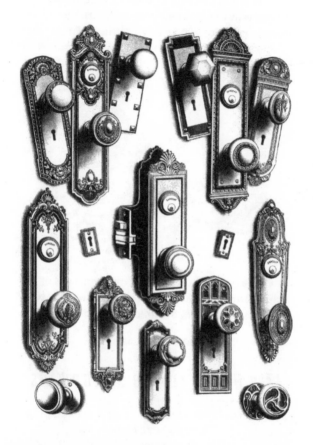

When I was around 10 years old I went to my school one Sunday afternoon and shoved pebbles into all the door locks so the doors couldn't be unlocked on Monday morning.

FAMILY

My dad was a music journalist. He tape-recorded
an interview with Bob Marley in the 1970s. My dad was
offered thousands of pounds for the recording in recent
years. I don't have the heart to tell him I recorded
over it with 'Tour de France' by Kraftwerk.

**My kids have taken to rating my meals out of 10
each and every night. It's all I can manage not to tell
them to fuck off, the ungrateful little shits.**

Life Hacks to Use on the Kids

*Parenting tips. What is this book now? A self-help guide?
Lord give us strength.*

I've trained my son to insist on special days like Father's Day
or my birthday that he needs to buy me a pint of beer in the
pub. I insist on a half. The pub staff always upgrade it to a full
pint free of charge when he pays, because he's four years old.

I regularly rub the dates off things like yoghurts in my child's packed lunch box if they've gone over, because eight-year-olds can be judgemental little shites.

RT: 91 FAV: 3,774

I hate kids. If there's a particularly annoying one when I'm out shopping, I'll sneak chocolate, sweets and similar items into their parents' trolley so the annoying little shitbag gets a bollocking from their parents at the checkout for trying to be sneaky.

RT: 226 FAV: 2,705

I have 3 kids. I routinely knock their tackiest junk toys under the sofa. If they don't look for them or ask where they are, I bin 'em a week later.

RT: 113 FAV: 2,555

I have a broken modem power supply I plug in sometimes to get the kids off the internet. I make them play board games with me and they have to read books and watch normal telly. These are my favourite evenings.

RT: 52 FAV: 2,206

Every Saturday and Sunday I ask my 3-year-old if she wants to go to nursery. When she says no, I say, 'OK, Daddy will let you stay at home today.' She thinks I'm awesome.

RT: 173 FAV: 8,027

FAMILY

Every weekend, I offer to go and do the tedious weekly shop.
I actually order it click and collect & then spend an hour sitting in
a cafe enjoying a coffee and breakfast in peace without my kids.

RT: 170 FAV: 8,305

When my son was 3, he said 'Oh fuck' when he
dropped a sandwich. I said, 'You can say that word,
it's fine, but never say "bell-bottom trousers".'
He immediately ran to the front door and screamed
'bell-bottom trousers' down the street.
Used it for years until someone put him wise.

RT: 128 FAV: 4,475

The Joy of Playing
Minor Pranks on Family

*Dad jokes territory really, but family are a captive
audience for jokes, so take advantage.*

~~~~

Every year I send my parents a Christmas card from
a made-up family and they have the same discussion
every year about how they may know them and they feel
bad that they never send a card back. Been doing it for
15 years now and won't stop.

RT: 290 FAV: 3,221

I changed the picture on my elderly mother's bus pass for
a picture of the ex-footballer John Fashanu. She happily
travelled every day for 6 months as a Premier League player
before being questioned by an eagle-eyed driver.

RT: 55 FAV: 2,552

My wife & I split up amicably and she has gone to live her parents while I sell the house. I've been digging a hole in my back garden over the last few nights just to wind up the neighbours.

RT: 584 FAV: 132

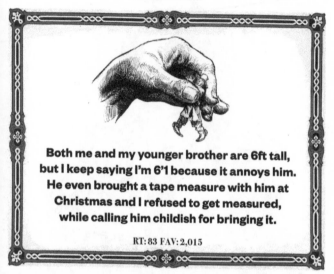

Both me and my younger brother are 6ft tall, but I keep saying I'm 6'1 because it annoys him. He even brought a tape measure with him at Christmas and I refused to get measured, while calling him childish for bringing it.

RT: 83 FAV: 2,015

Last year for April Fools, I let myself into Mum's house and took her car keys. Planned to hide the car round the corner. While driving away I hit 3 cars, panicked and drove off into town. I abandoned the car and keys.
Mum reported the car stolen and I never owned up.

RT: 180 FAV: 4,979

My dad's confession really, but... In the 80s we lived next door to a pet shop that put a parrot in a cage at the front of the shop. My dad would walk past with his dogs and say 'Piss off' to it at least eight times a day. The shop had to retire the parrot for swearing at people.

RT: 86 FAV: 2,458

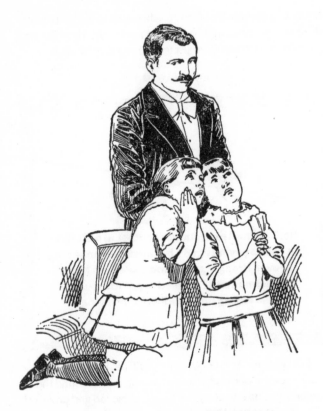

I convinced my two young children
that I invented cheese, the spiky bits on
pineapples, daytime and the name Stuart.
I forgot about it and several months later,
my daughter came home from school and
informed me that her teacher had said: 'Your
father didn't invent cheese or daytime.'

My brother found a laptop on a train and planned to sell it to a mate of mine. I changed the screensaver to come on after 15 secs with the words 'This laptop is fitted with a tracking device. Police are aware of its location.' He threw it in the canal in a panic. Thieving twat.

RT: 56 FAV: 2,237

My sister always sends me photos of her kids and asks me to Photoshop other people out. I've been doing this for a while, but I add Ainsley Harriott's face into the bushes or trees and she hasn't noticed yet despite printing them.

RT: 535 FAV: 16.2K

Skanky Dads Who Try and Get You Into Theme Parks Without Paying Are the Best

Are you even a dad if you're not trying to do it on the cheap?

On days out with the family, I wear a high-vis to enter for free as no-one questions someone in high-vis. My wife moans when she realises I've only booked her and the kids tickets. 5 years and I've only been stopped once – at Alton Towers, because I didn't have my face mask on.

RT: 69 FAV: 2,447

My dad used to take us to Alton Towers every year. He always hid all three of us kids in the boot and only paid at the gate for two adults. We were told to keep quiet or else, and always parked in the furthest corner of the car park to get out.

My dad once got me, my sister and a friend into a local amusement park for free by telling them we were Barnardo's orphans on a day trip out.

Dad Jokes

~~~~~~

Dad jokes are passed from father to son, rather like male-pattern baldness and a propensity to complain that 'this place isn't a bloody hotel you know'.

~~~~

Whenever I've been at an international airport over the past 40 years, I've stood at the departure boards & said: 'New York, London, Paris, Munich, everybody talk about mmm Pop Music.' Last week, a smartly dressed man replied, 'Shoobie doobie do wop.' Mission accomplished.

I've started calling my wife's right breast Boris as they're both right tits. She hates me.

Aged 6 or 7, I did the Spot the Ball competition in the paper with my dad, sticking a pin in the page where I thought the concealed football should be. My dad told me I would have guessed correctly when I heard a PFFFT noise. I was 30 when I realised I'd been had.

My first words upon waking up after brain surgery were 'What's up you slaaaags' in a shit, mumbled cockney accent. I've used the nurse's explanation that it was 'post-surgery grogginess' as an excuse for years, but the truth is I was pretty lucid and just thought it was funny.

When someone thanks me for a piece of work I say 'Jizz!' so it sounds like 'Cheers!' said quickly. I've done this for 10+ years & no one has ever picked me up on it, as they will probably never say, 'Sorry, did you say Jizz?' If they do, I will say, 'No, I said Cheers, why would I say Jizz?'

Signs That You Are Ageing

~~~~~~

We're all getting older but remember, the alternative is worse: death.

~~~~

I'm 47. Was telling a young colleague about *Brass Eye* and *The Day Today*, and said, 'I can lend you the DVDs if you like.' His derisory snort made me realise what a dreadfully sad old donkey I have become. Never felt so old.

FAMILY

After stumbling on to a naked beach, I am terrified
about what ageing will do to my balls.

**My wife asked why I was so down and if it was
something she had done. I told her I was struggling at
work – it's actually because I realised I am now so old
that I have had to retire from professional football
in my own daydreams. Sad times.**

As I get older, I find myself enjoying the music of Celine Dion,
Simply Red & Phil Collins a lot more than I feel I should. I'm 42
and still love lots of new music, but I find stuff like Collins is
a comfort blanket of sorts.

**I've recently started wiping my arse before bed.
I've not had a dump or anything; I guess it's just the
stains from farting all day. Try it, you'll be surprised!**

My mates and I played football all the time as kids.
Then, without knowing it, we once played together for
the final time. I think about this often and it breaks
my ageing heart that we've all grown up.

I profess to hate everything about getting
older while quietly enjoying the general
acceptance of my grumpiness and being
pathetically excited about my imminent
free bus pass, even though I hate buses.

As I get older, I've noticed my farts have dropped a couple of octaves... I often wonder whether that has been a direct result of age, or my wife pegging me.

Subcommandment:
Thou Shalt Love and Honour
Your Elderly Parents

You'll miss the UKIP-y old bastards when they're gone. Forgive them for their views, for your views too will be decried as terrible once you're this age.

~~~~

When I'm going to call my mum, I always wait until no more than 30 minutes before one of her TV programmes is starting so the call doesn't go on too long. There's only so much gossip from her village that I can bear to listen to.

My father has refused to pay the TV licence in a protest against 'The BBC', but my poor mother is in a state of constant stress, thinking they will get a knock on the door and be fined. So I secretly pay the licence fee. I need to tell Mum, though.

RT: 168 FAV: 5,289

I'm a 45-year-old bloke and when I visit my parents I take a bag of washing with me. They don't know that it's not always dirty; I do it so I have something that smells like my mum and dad's house, because I miss them sometimes when I'm not there.

RT: 294 FAV: 9,688

I visit my mother monthly and get my hair cut straight afterwards because otherwise she tells me off for cutting it too short. I am a 50-year-old senior manager. I shouldn't have to do this.

RT: 33 FAV: 2,529

When my father is reading my son a story, I sit in the room on my phone and pretend to scroll. But I really enjoying listening to them. Reminds me of my own childhood.

RT: 97 FAV: 7,223

My dad set up a monthly direct debit of £50 to me when I was a student. I guess he forgot to cancel it because it's still in place. I left university 25 years ago and have my own mortgage and family; some months, that £50 has meant we don't go completely to the wall.

I've worked with my dad for 27 years. He's 75 now, works 1 day a week, but doesn't really do much. I love having him around, so once a month I send him in to clients I've already done the deal with to do the paperwork. He loves being involved & they love our family ethos.

My mother was in hospital when her goldfish died. I didn't want to make things worse for her, so replaced the fish. 3 years later that fish died and I didn't want Mum upset so replaced again. Now Mum's 80 and she thinks her fish is 14.

My mum has dementia and was getting very upset that she kept forgetting where she put her cigarette lighter. I bought 80 of them. They are now in every coat, drawer and pocket. She's so happy when she says 'I remembered!' It makes me smile that she's happy.

Bittersweet Feelings About Dead People

~~~~~~

This section is for all the loved ones who are no longer with us, including this compiler's dad, who would have likely found this whole project quite amusing.

~~~~

My dad always followed a specific football team's scores. I thought he supported them and followed suit. Turns out he checked the results so he'd have something to talk about with some chap at work. I now support a team because of someone called Clive that I've never met.

RT: 324 FAV: 106

My husband's dying wish was to make people think he led a double life. We had 3 blacked-out Land Rovers follow the cortege and actors in suits and trench coats 'observe' the funeral from a distance – he was a bank manager for TSB and to this day I haven't told anyone the truth.

RT: 3,437 FAV: 39.1K

My best mate killed himself during lockdown. I did the porn buddy thing. Sneaking his fleshlights & electric butt plugs out of his house under the noses of his grieving parents and taking them to the tip was simultaneously the saddest and funniest thing I've ever had to do.

RT: 250 FAV: 3,654

Before my dad passed away, we had some very heated debates on whether Boris Johnson would make a good prime minister. I miss him for so many reasons, but right now I'm gutted that I don't have the chance to say, 'Told you so, Dad.'

I had an argument with my dad before he died about a sander he said I'd borrowed. I swore I didn't have it. I did, I just couldn't find it. 5 years later, I found it. If there's an afterlife, Dad, where did you keep the sanding sheets? Knock once for the garage, twice for the shed.

My mum died. I still send her photos and WhatsApp messages about my day. When I visit my dad, I stick her phone on charge and load WhatsApp there, so that on my phone, it looks as though they've been read.

My dad died 10 years ago. I still message him every birthday. His number has now been recycled and the new owner is female. She gets quite irate every June 15th.

I sometimes find myself watching old TV comedy shows online – *Rising Damp, The Brittas Empire,* etc – not because I like them so much, but because they remind me of how my father used to howl with laughter at them. He died 16 years ago.

For 30 years, I've added a single grain of coffee into every cup of tea I make because my mum once claimed she could taste 'when I stir your father's coffee first'. She never caught on. It's 5 years since she passed and I still make tea with a single grain of coffee. Miss you, Mum x.

I go on Google Maps to the images that are dated as being taken before my dad died so I can walk around a little bit in a world where he is still with me.

My mother recently cleaned out my uncle's house after he moved into an assisted living home. It was a mess. Inside the mess, she found a silver canister. Inside were someone's ashes. We are not sure whose. I took them and spread them in the pond of a local park. RIP someone.

When I was 16, my dad sat me down and told me I had an older brother who died of cot death before I was born. They had a little box of his stuff, wrist band and his birth certificate. I nicked the birth cert every weekend to get served in pubs in town. Figured my bro wouldn't mind.

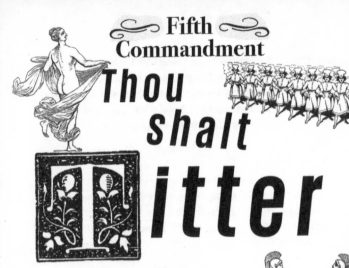

Fifth Commandment

Thou shalt Titter

at stuff about

Sex

Apparently the British are ashamed about sex.
Bollocks. You're all rutting like common animals.
And with common animals.

Anyone remember them little hats on the Innocent smoothie bottles? I collected them years ago and was about to throw them out until one day I decided to put one over my bellend for a laugh. I realised it's so warm and cosy, I now wear them through the cold winter months.

RT: 0 FAV: 2,186

I'd really like to try a threesome, but even if my wife did agree, I suspect I would have no idea what to do in the situation and would probably end up in the kitchen eating a sandwich.

RT: 261 FAV: 3,576

Went on a date, ended up snogging, got a £6 taxi back to hers, only had a £20 so, in my horny haste, told the driver to keep the change. Got out of the cab and she revealed to me she had a boyfriend. Gutted, I left. Still bitter about it, but more so about the £14 tip.

RT: 86 FAV: 2,716

Staying at a friend's house, I slept on the floor while he and his girlfriend were in the bed. Woke up in the night to hear her tossing him off while whispering the dirtiest, filthiest words of encouragement. Never been more jealous of someone in my life.

RT: 25 FAV: 2,344

My husband and I have been together for nearly 23 years. Still absolutely crazy about him, and I still fancy him. Every time he gets out of bed in the morning, I take a good look at his cock and arse as he is putting on his dressing gown, and it makes me feel good.

Watching some porn I came across a category called 'small dick'. Thought I'd watch it to give myself a laugh. At least 90% of them on there have bigger dicks than mine. Gutted.

After one too many bevvies at a Pontins 80s weekender in Southport, I ended up having a threesome with a married couple. She wanted railing, he wanted a dildo up the arse simultaneously. Worst part was going into work on the Monday and locking eyes with the new tech support guy.

Slept with someone new recently. Looked at our phones afterwards and were amazed by how long we'd been at it. She was all admiring, and I felt like a proper stud. Then we realised that while we'd been fucking, the clocks had gone forward an hour.

I once woke up in a random girl's bed after a one-night stand, with no recollection of the night before. I stumbled to the bathroom for a piss and was surprised not to hear any splash. I glanced down and realised I was filling up a condom like a water balloon.

Sex Tips

~~~~~~

Imagine this bit is like reading the sex tips in Cosmo
and you're still 14, OK?

~~~~

**Had a hot date, so ate a tonne of watermelon beforehand
as I'd read it helps you get super hard. Ended up having
to cut the evening short because it went right through
me & I couldn't stop shitting.**

RT: 230 FAV: 6,731

If I think I'm going to jizz too soon during sex, to take my
mind off it & delay I nearly always resort to thinking
about Liverpool FC's starting 11 and the squad tactics.
Once a woman asked why she could hear me muttering the
words 'Gini Wijnaldum'. I still came too soon.

RT: 242 FAV: 2,544

**After too much wine, my wife and I tried fisting.
Would not recommend. 1 star.**

RT: 245 FAV: 3,226

During the first lockdown, me and my partner would
shag every Thursday evening and time our orgasms for
when the clapping started. We'd pretend it was for us.

RT: 401 FAV: 476

Your teenage years would be so much easier if people didn't make such a big deal about losing your virginity. Like, nothing changed in my life afterwards apart from knowing that Lucy from my Media class had a weird mole next to her fanny.

RT: 184 FAV: 3,736

I'm a sex worker and when I found an enlarged prostate, I encouraged the client to go and see a doctor. Don't be scared to do bum stuff, guys; it might save your life.

RT: 120 FAV: 2,876

Failed Attempts to Be Sexy

~~~~~~

If you're having impure thoughts about that sexy bin man (hello Jo), just have a quick read of this to make your sex bits heal up in shame.

~~~~

I once secretly rubbed an ice cube all over myself while in a nightclub in an attempt to give myself a sexy wet glistening look in front of a bloke I fancied. When I went to the loo, he asked my friend if I was going through the menopause. I was 25.

RT: 115 FAV: 4,287

Having two young kids, we need to sneak in nooky when possible. One morning we were in the middle of some tomfoolery when we were interrupted by our eldest. He jumped into bed with us but then insisted he could smell the ocean. Needless to say, we quickly adjourned for breakfast.

RT: 58 FAV: 2,397

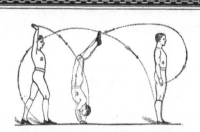

I'm quite vanilla in the bedroom, so when my girlfriend asked, I said I was 'kinda into feet' as it was the first thing that came to mind. Now she's my wife of 8 years she gives me regular foot jobs, which I don't really want and are honestly quite underwhelming.

RT: 184 FAV: 3,957

Cooked a romantic dinner, after which me and my partner proceeded to have some fun. Within 5 minutes she was in the bath, legs in the air, washing her vagina with milk. I still had chillies on my fingers from cooking the dinner.

RT: 270 FAV: 4,888

I'm really bad at dirty talk and while my other half was fingering me, I told him to 'put some welly into it'. The shock to him was such that he stopped it and gave me a look that can only be described as pure bewilderment. Sorry darling.

RT: 8 FAV: 3,733

My wife gives the worst hand jobs. It feels like she's going to pull my dick off. But I can't think of a way to tactfully address this. We've been together fifteen years. My poor penis.

RT: 322 FAV: 3,014

I blocked a guy on Grindr after a couple of exchanges. Only because he said he was having dirty 'faults' rather than 'thoughts'. I can't shag the thick.

Met a guy at the park walking the dogs. He walked his there at the same time. We decided to come back to mine to fool about. After we finished I showed him out. I couldn't find 2 of the condoms we used. Found them the next morning. My dogs shat them out. At the park.

Today I had my first naked tantra massage. At the end, the masseuse told me the hygiene around my arsehole needed improvement. Not the happy ending I was looking for.

My Dutch girlfriend sucked me off, then spat it into a pan and fried it. It's not really a confession, more an unburdening.

Wanking Corner

~~~~~~

Our critics say Fesshole is mostly stories about masturbation. Correct.

~~~~

I left my model train magazine in the masturbation room at the fertility clinic. I couldn't ask for it back – I was too embarrassed they'd think I'd been wanking to miniature locomotives.

**Told my husband it really turns me
on to watch him wank. It doesn't.
But saves me from having to do it.**

My wife keeps deleting the browser history and cookies on my iPad after watching porn. The only reason I know is my Wordle streak keeps resetting and it's getting frustrating.

RT: 0 FAV: 3,746

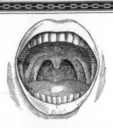

Last night I had a furious wank over what I thought was the sound of my flatmate going at it with her vibrator but turned out to be one of the electric toothbrushes that had fallen into the sink.

RT: 69 FAV: 2,681

Other half uses my expensive body lotion when he wanks. I've nothing against him wanking, but it royally pisses me off he uses my cream then denies it. So I've just filled an empty tub with cheap hair-removal cream.

RT: 106 FAV: 4,730

I leave a cheap bottle of moisturiser next to our en suite toilet so my husband doesn't use my expensive stuff for his ridiculous lockdown masturbation habit. No one needs that many 10 minute poos, Allan.

RT: 171 FAV: 2,392

I'm about to live alone for the first time at 28. I'm genuinely scared I'm going to wank myself to death.

RT: 337 FAV: 4,755

Since discovering my porn internet history on my laptop – and the associated fall-out – my wife now thinks I need to be 'serviced' every night. I honestly can't be fucked with it. I just want a good wank.

My husband prefers being wanked off to full sex, which I'm fine with, except for the arm pain. I've tried many songs to keep myself in rhythm and focused, and have landed on 'Stop' by the Spice Girls as the best wanking beat.

I'm a plumber, once was watching porn, about to rub one out and instantly lost my boner when I saw the absolutely atrocious copper pipework in the background.

First night in a new house, heard the neighbours getting it on. Her moaning and groaning started to get to me, so much so that I had a cheeky wank. Turns out she was in labour with her third child.

SEX

The Embarrassment of Sex and Your Parents Existing in the Same Universe

~~~~~~

Aged 13, your editor once called our dad a wanker and our mum said, 'No Rob, YOU'RE the wanker.' She knew! Our secret shame!

~~~~

I got a video recorder when I was 14. I'd connect mine to the one downstairs and copied all my dad's pornos. One was about aliens and they whistled a tune instead of speaking. One morning I came downstairs whistling the tune, and my dad said, 'Where've I heard that before?'

RT: 188 FAV: 4,803

When I was 15, I discovered a VHS tape of a my parents having a sex party with 2 other couples. Sold it for £5 and some Panini stickers. World Cup special-edition stickers, I am not an idiot.

RT: 146 FAV: 2,450

Came home on a midnight train to surprise my folks at the start of uni holidays once. Heard my dad yelling for my mum to 'do my arse harder' to the 'empty' house. I will never unhear anything from that night. They know I know. We've never discussed it.

Meeting my wife's father for the first time: I went in for a handshake, he went in for a hug. The result was his earlobe making its way into my open mouth, where I tickled it with my tongue. We've never mentioned it and it's been 15 years. It's buried deep.

I was caught at school with weed. My dad freaked out and decided to burn all his pornography before the police turned up to raid the house. We sat together and watched it burn in silence. It's the closest we've ever been. The police never showed up.

Sex Boasts

~~~~~~

Can everyone stop sending in their sex boasts?
We haven't had sex since 1998 and we're getting jealous.

~~~~

**God blessed me with a huge thingy and also a face
the tide wouldn't take out. I needed ways to show
off what I had. I joined local swimming and athletics
clubs so I could wear lycra. It wasn't long before
I became really popular. Shame on you, girls.**

RT: 204 FAV: 4,055

Aged 18, my girlfriend and I were in an online chat room with
some guy when he suddenly suggested she should try anal
with me. She did. 20 years later, it's still an occasional treat.
Thanks, weird internet guy!

RT: 115 FAV: 2,827

**My maths teacher didn't like me at school. Years later,
I bumped into his daughter at university. One thing led
to another and I ended up going back to her place. The
most enjoyable part of the encounter was imagining how
cross he would be that I was shagging his daughter.**

RT: 142 FAV: 4,498

My smartwatch logs any kind of repetitive hand
movements as steps. It takes 600 steps to bring my wife
to orgasm, on average. Our record is 247 steps.

RT: 97 FAV: 2,738

A couple of years ago, I took a Viagra and half an E in the expectation of a night of filthy sex with my mistress. She cancelled at short notice so my wife bore the brunt of it. I've been happily married, faithful and fulfilled since.

I was once duped into visiting a brothel by a group of friends after a night out. Not up my street at all. After each friend had gone into a room with one of the ladies, I spent the night sitting with the madam drinking tea and watching repeats of *Catchphrase*. I had a great time!

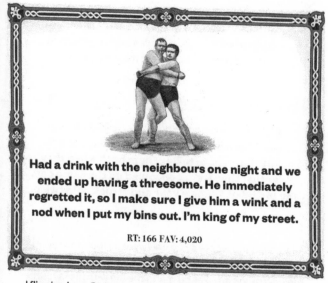

Had a drink with the neighbours one night and we ended up having a threesome. He immediately regretted it, so I make sure I give him a wink and a nod when I put my bins out. I'm king of my street.

I flipping love *Strictly Come Dancing*. My wife gets so horny watching the men prance around that it's a guaranteed blo – I get a stonk-on when the trumpets start playing. Long may it continue.

I slept with a prostitute once. When I arrived, she had her PlayStation on and now we are PSN friends.

I pretended to be deaf in the uni library to avoid a questionnaire. One thing led to another, ended up in bed with the girl that was asking questions, had to pretend to be deaf the whole night.

My 3-year-old son and 1-year-old daughter were born in the same month, 2 days apart. Looking forward to telling them both when they're older that they were conceived on the same day, my birthday. 1 shag a year and struck gold twice.

My husband works away one week in four and I send him saucy videos while he's away. He delights in telling me how much smaller he made the file with his favourite compression software, so I make sure the files are extra big so he feels extra good.

Gay (I Am 100% Straight)

~~~~~~

These people are keen to tell you that they're firmly heterosexual.

~~~~

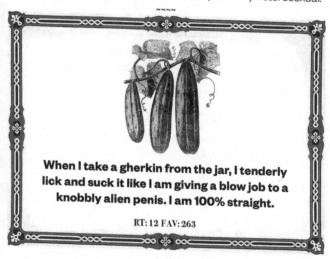

When I take a gherkin from the jar, I tenderly lick and suck it like I am giving a blow job to a knobbly alien penis. I am 100% straight.

RT: 12 FAV: 263

After I split up with my first girlfriend, I went for a drive and parked up at beauty spot to get some fresh air after crying my eyes out. Didn't know that it was actually a gay hook-up spot. Random guy came over to me and asked if he could suck me off. Best blow job I ever had.

RT: 304 FAV: 3,921

I am straight. I went to a gay man to have my back waxed. Once he'd done that, he suggested doing my chest hair, then wet-shaving my junk. There was A LOT of unnecessary handling, and I got a raging hard-on. We didn't mention it. I'd probably go back.

RT: 222 FAV: 2,989

I sometimes put blobs of my girlfriend's conditioner in my beard so it looks like I've just sucked a guy off. I'm 100% straight.

I'm not gay, but I did spend one week-long cycling trip shagging guys on Grindr because I didn't want to pay for hotels and needed a place to stay for the night. Would do it again.

Always thought I was straight, but during lockdown got thinking about what it would be like to have sex with men. Tried it, loved it, not going back. Turns out maybe I'm not straight.

Men – Don't Be Creepy Arseholes, OK?

Men. You. Need. To. Stop. (And get therapy.)

I run successful social media accounts on nursing – completely androgynous, anomalous and professional, but the amount of suggestive DMs from men is ridiculous! I'm a male charge nurse, you twats. Stop it or I'm publishing them.

I've got a fake female profile on Facebook; it's from a 12-year-old account and quite convincing. I regularly get creepy messages from men and I play along a little, then if they're in a relationship, I screenshot the conversation to their partner. Everyone needs a hobby.

RT: 174 FAV: 5,672

Female, 28, and got a body cam to film arseholes abusing me while out running. Local NPT love visiting people at home if I get a number plate. So far I've had 2 charged and 1 guy lost his job, and I've no regrets.

RT: 594 FAV: 8,385

Women Who Aren't 100% Sure About Their Sexy Hunk of a Man

~~~~~~

Women. You know the best option is to give up on men. Someone else will probably take them on, like a rescue dog.

~~~~

My husband has just purchased the most hideous pair of boots that I've ever seen in my life and quite frankly, I'm not sure we'll ever have sex again.

RT: 179 FAV: 2,851

I've been secretly sexting a man twice my age and it's hot af except his spelling is terrible: he said he was going to take me to Narnia. I think he meant nirvana.

RT: 544 FAV: 4,998

My husband insists on showing me how small his penis gets every time after he exercises. I try to be supportive but it looks like a thumb and is a major turn-off.

RT: 198 FAV: 2,379

I've stopped giving my partner head, as they've switched to using Imperial Leather soap to wash themselves and the scent & taste of their cock reminds me of my grandparents, which knocks me out the mood faster than you can say 'Werther's Original'.

RT: 316 FAV: 4,630

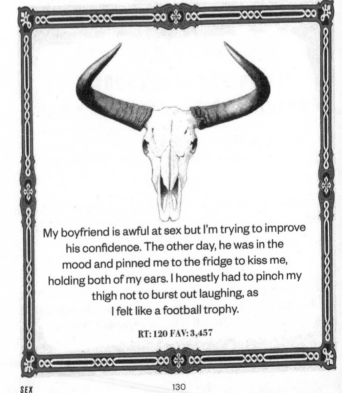

My boyfriend is awful at sex but I'm trying to improve his confidence. The other day, he was in the mood and pinned me to the fridge to kiss me, holding both of my ears. I honestly had to pinch my thigh not to burst out laughing, as I felt like a football trophy.

RT: 120 FAV: 3,457

READERS' WANK FANTASIES

One of the terrible things about running Fesshole is that people endlessly submit who they fancy. We generally don't tweet this out so the whole thing doesn't turn into cyber-Razzle, but as we get one chance at a book, let humanity learn from these mistakes. Here are the people you lust after – and you won't stop shouting about it. And oddly, you've all got the horn for Tory MPs. Frankly, all of you need a cold shower and a donk with a spoon.

Top Three Men
3. Dominic Cummings
'I fancy Dominic Cummings. I don't like him, but there's something about the fact he doesn't give a shit I find massively attractive. Anyone else?!'
2. Matt Hancock
'After the Matt Hancock video came out I developed a real crush on him. Went through a stage of thinking about him while having sex with my husband.'
1. Dominic Raab
'I'm a good-looking, intelligent, leftie, socialist woman, but I sometimes masturbate imagining Dominic Raab is shagging me.'

Top Three Women
3. Liz Truss
'I secretly want to shag Liz Truss while she tells me about pork markets.'
2. Nadine Dorries
'I really, really fancy Nadine Dorries. The only reason I'm confessing this is that I know there must be others in the same boat as me and I want them to know they're not alone.'
1. Priti Patel
'I hate myself for thinking Priti Patel is kinda hot. That stern, glasses-wearing, neo-fascist thing seems to do it for me. I sometimes fantasise about her threatening to deport me while she angrily rides me.'

Apologies if you're reading this bit years after this book was published, as nothing that dates as quickly as yesterday's politicians. Look them up on Wikipedia using your VR glasses while you're hiding from climate change.

Sixth Commandment

Thou shalt have Relationships because the alternative is worse...

Love is pissing your partner's shit stains off the toilet.

My wife and I chat to each other all day on shared Google Sheets so it looks like we're working.

RT: 123 FAV: 3,642

I am a secret knitter. My girlfriend is pregnant and I've had to invent an old lady at work who I attribute all the knitted garments to. I've even called her Nora. I fucking love knitting.

RT: 468 FAV: 5,546

Found a wallet long ago. Stuffed with cash. Owner easily found on social media. Read his posts & it was full of abuse about the football team I support. Booked a weekend away at a swanky hotel. Proposed to the girl who is now my wife.

RT: 272 FAV: 7,352

Every night in bed, without fail, my girlfriend and I reverse into each other and ritualistically touch bums just before we nod off. It's the most important part of our routine. I wish I could tell everyone how happy it makes me but I'd sound a bit weird.

RT: 358 FAV: 9,249

On our anniversary and sometimes for Valentine's, my husband buys me expensive flowers from the florist. I wish he wouldn't, and would instead book us into a hotel so we can have lots of noisy sex without worrying about the kids.

RT: 238 FAV: 2,762

I was on my laptop last night when my wife told me to turn it off, as she could see my work was just upsetting me. I didn't like to tell her my team on Football Manager had just suffered a particularly distressing 5–2 defeat.

RT: 297 FAV: 6,092

How We Met

~~~~~~

Romance is not dead on Fesshole. Here's some lovely stories of how these good people met. And if you're single and looking for love – never give up on your dreams. Or more practically, lower your standards, until someone says, 'OK, I suppose.'

~~~~

About 20 years ago, I dumped this girl because I didn't particularly like her. She continued to email me erotic messages and once, feeling bored and horny, I replied and we went out and ended up having sex. Four kids later we're still together, and I still don't like her.

RT: 293 FAV: 4,446

Years ago, I was moaning about
being single to my sis and she asked
which of her mates I fancied – I said 'Cath',
and she rang her to arrange a date.
We've been together for 15 years now.
The 'Cath' my sis rang wasn't the one I meant.

I once asked a girl out and she said she doesn't like men with beards. I said I have a beard to cover a skin condition on my jaw. She felt guilty and gave me a pity date. It went well and we've been together for 3 years. But now I can never shave it off.

I mounted the curb while driving and clipped a wall. I was looking at the girl on the other side of the road.
I told her and the policeman I swerved to miss a fox.
We've now been married 17 years.

Really liked this girl on a night out and my friend noticed. He gave her my number and we texted for a while before we finally met. Turned out he gave it to the wrong girl. Been together for 5 years now and all is well, but she must never know .

I once climbed out of a window to escape a boring date.
Sadly the window led to a dead-end courtyard. After a struggle I climbed back in and told my date I'd been a while due to taking a big shit. We've now been together 18 months.

My wife and I met through mutual friends years before we got together, but I was too shy to talk to her. Even mentioned it in my wedding speech. Recently a friend put some photos of the night in question on Facebook. Turns out it was a similar-looking but entirely different girl.

My then-girlfriend was hassling me to get married. I only agreed as my family's marriage record was terrible and I assumed this would be the same, and it would only last a short time, like everyone else's. We've been married for 36 years now.

In 2002, I borrowed a book from Leeds Central Library. It was geeky and architectural and someone had left a printed email in the middle of the book. It was sweet, I emailed, we married and had kids. Without books I'd probably be a spinster.

I once read an article about a woman who said 'yes' to anyone who asked her out on a date for a year. That week, a guy asked me out at a bar. I didn't fancy him at all but I remembered the article and said yes. We've been married 7 years. I've never told him.

Brilliant Flirting

~~~~~~

Don't you wish that office crush was a little bit more?
Stop it, Steve, it'll never happen.

~~~~

**I planned to get a tattoo and looked online
in my local area. I found someone to tattoo me; turns
out she's the most amazing woman I've ever
encountered. I've had 2 legs covered and still
don't have the balls to tell her I really fancy her.**

RT: 28 FAV: 2,972

Met the woman of my dreams at a party. We flirted and
exchanged numbers. Before I could call her, I had to go
to hospital with suspected appendicitis. She was the duty
surgeon and had to carry out a rectal exam while a male
chaperone nurse watched. Couldn't call her after that.

RT: 288 FAV: 3,870

**Was tipsy at a restaurant & flirting with a cute waiter.
I wrote my number on a paper napkin,
put it in my pocket & later handed it to him saying,
'Here, use it sometime' & left. Next day found
the napkin in my pocket. Must've given him a
used tissue. Never went back there again.**

RT: 88 FAV: 4,539

I've started going to a chess club because a girl I fancy wanted to go. I now spend one evening a week being beaten by old men at a game I find boring, in the hope of sex.

RELATIONSHIPS

Overheard a girl I fancied on my train talking to her friend about how men are all the same: always on their phones. From that day forward I've carried a book to try and impress her. Been reading *Grapes of Wrath* for two months now and a shit book. Never seen her since.

Met a girl years ago through work. Fell head over heels in love with her but never did anything about it. Did once send her flowers anonymously for Valentine's. She thought they came from someone else, and now they're married. Absolutely kills me that I did this.

Yesterday when bemoaning her latest failed relationship, my attractive 30-year-old intern squeezed my arm and said, 'God I wish I could clone you.' I'm a chubby bloke in his 50s and very loyal to my wife, but that arm squeeze has gone right into the spank bank.

Pre-mobiles, I met a girl on holiday. We planned to meet in the UK at an M3 service station midway between us. I waited but she never showed. When leaving, I realised that she might have been in the mirror-image service station on the other side of the road. Regret it to this day.

There's a woman at work I have a major crush on. The printer is in my office and 9 times out of 10, it's her who has printed something that she'll come to collect. It's at a point now where the sound of a printer going off makes me hard.

RT: 180 FAV: 2,269

I've volunteered at a foodbank for over a year. I originally went in for food but the girl working there was too good-looking to admit that to, so I said I'd come to help out instead.

RT: 94 FAV: 2,204

Life Hacks From Women to Use On Men

Men are stupidly easy to manipulate. It's because half of their brain is idling on Football Manager at all times. Or Duran Duran B-sides if they're not sporty.

~~~~

I regularly buy really expensive handbags. My partner wonders how much they are and I tell him I get them for about £2 in a charity shop. He's none the wiser.

RT: 65 FAV: 1,329

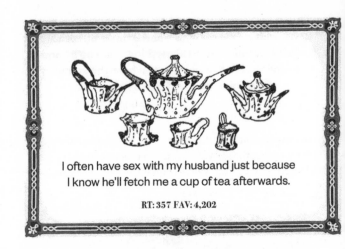

I often have sex with my husband just because
I know he'll fetch me a cup of tea afterwards.

RT: 357 FAV: 4,202

**I deliberately make my husband a nice big drink
before bed. That way, I know he's going to get up
in the night for a wee, and will also let the dog out
for a wee. I stay in bed, comfy and warm.**

RT: 112 FAV: 6,807

I hired a cleaner after my partner refused to help and now
every Friday night my partner treats me to takeaway
and flowers for cleaning the house. A year later, I'm
starting to feel slightly guilty. Is it too late to fess up?

RT: 202 FAV: 2,336

**One winter, my bf complained about how chapped
and sore his hands were but he refused to use
hand cream. Every night while he slept, I moisturised
his left hand. After a month he exclaimed his left hand
was healed but his right was still sore. I fessed up.
He now uses moisturiser.**

RT: 56 FAV: 3,748

Despite both of us working full-time, I still do the lion's share of the domestic tasks. Fed up of arguing about it, so I just do it now. Every week when I do the weekly food shop at Asda, I buy a £25 John Lewis voucher on the joint account as compensation for my time.

RT: 645 FAV: 203

Husband can't be arsed to empty his pockets when putting clothes in the wash basket. I keep all cash I find. His laziness has funded a spa break for me and a friend.

RT: 103 FAV: 6,344

Life Hacks From Men to Use On Women

~~~~~~

Lying is only evil if it's used for evil. If it's just to make the home life slightly more bearable, it's morally fine.

~~~~

When the wife is horny but I'm not up for it, I kill the moment by dirty talking in a Jimmy Savile voice. Does the trick every time. Now then, now then.

RT: 239 FAV: 3,085

If my wife puts on a TV show I don't want to watch, I tell her I fancy one of the women in it . She'll turn it off and tell me she'll watch it when I'm not home.

RT: 133 FAV: 3,038

Wife insists on decluttering only through giving away on Gumtree, even the smallest shit. It takes too long. I make fake accounts, arrange for things to be left for pick-up and throw them away without her knowledge.

RT: 91 FAV: 2,177

I go for a pint & rum on my Saturday dog walk.
I always just sit by myself, but to justify it, I tell my wife
I'm meeting 'Jim'. Jim doesn't exist & never has.
It's my little time to be alone & happy.
Bollocks to it, all blokes should try it.

RT: 384 FAV: 5,287

My wife wanted an awful first name for our son while she was expecting him, so I bribed my brother to adopt a dog from a shelter and give it the same name. Did the trick, and brother loves being a dog owner, so all good.

RT: 174 FAV: 3,918

I pretend to the missus that my electric car needs somebody to sit in it for at least an hour daily with the key to charge it up. It is the best hour of my day. I just watch Netflix on the drive away from her and the kids.

RT: 269 FAV: 4,470

I check my wife's phone when she's not looking, not to check if she's cheating, but to get present ideas. She's always shocked when I get what she wanted.

I wrote code to automatically send my girlfriend a 'good morning' text each morning, with a randomised affectionate greeting, number of kisses on the end and an emoji from a predefined set. Brownie points like you wouldn't believe.

My wife hated her job but wouldn't leave. I tarted up her CV, sent it off with a new email address that came to me. She got an interview, so I got a friend to ring her and pretend to be a head-hunter. She got the job and loves it.

I buy my dad, who's in his late seventies, top-quality tools for birthdays and Christmas. He appreciates them, but I'm also playing the long game. My wife would never let me buy expensive tools for myself.

Revenge On the Ex

*Content warning: please don't do anything like this.
Your best bet, when dealing with an ex, is to live well.
(And put their number in the local loos.)*

~~~~

When my ex broke my heart, I took a piece of Lego from each one of his Lego sets. He won't be complete without me and neither will his Lego. Still miss him.

RT: 335 FAV: 6,250

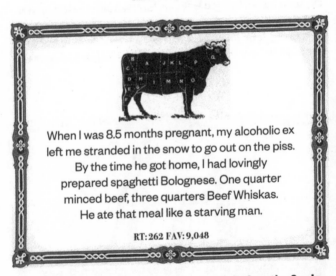

When I was 8.5 months pregnant, my alcoholic ex left me stranded in the snow to go out on the piss. By the time he got home, I had lovingly prepared spaghetti Bolognese. One quarter minced beef, three quarters Beef Whiskas. He ate that meal like a starving man.

RT: 262 FAV: 9,048

My ex broke up with me about a month before the finale of his favourite Netflix show hit. He'd organised a viewing party ready for midnight when it dropped. I let him stay signed in on my account until 11.59pm that day, when I changed the password & forced log-out on all devices.

RT: 761 FAV: 32.1K

I knew my ex was splitting up with me so I hid his passport by tucking it under his TV unit before I left. He won't think to look there, meaning he can't go on his lads' holiday this year as he'll leave everything to the night before.

My husband is having an affair. While biding my time to leave, I occasionally sneak one of his socks or underpants into the bin and take great pleasure in thanking him for taking it out on bin nights.

My dickhead ex blocked me on all forms of social media and messaging, so I now get to him by sending him 1p bank transfers with insults in the reference. Money well spent.

When I found out my now ex-boyfriend cheated on me, I went into his laptop and deleted the contents of his many saved porn folders, replacing them with instructions for various flat-pack furniture.

My husband is having an affair and won't leave as he owns half the house and still pays the bills. His mistress bought him some aftershave; I poured out half and pissed in the bottle to top it up. So every time he goes out wearing it, he stinks of piss.

My ex-boyfriend cheated on me with someone he worked with, so when a vacancy came up at the place they both worked, I applied just to scare them a bit. I wasted six hours on that application for a job I was never going to take. I just wanted to be petty.

RT: 36 FAV: 2,095

When my ex broke up with me, he left himself logged in to Facebook on my iPad. I occasionally go through his conversations and delete messages before he reads them. He has missed quite a few important things...

RT: 289 FAV: 6,103

I just got dumped, so I'm taking his CDs, books and the only copy of his MA thesis to Oxfam tomorrow.

RT: 334 FAV: 4,212

Split with the Mrs a few months ago as she was seeing someone else who she's now moved into our marital home. I still have the Hive heating app on my phone. I keep turning it up to maximum when they go to work. Hope it's costing them a fortune.

RT: 1,950 FAV: 58.4K

My ex has played the same numbers on the lottery for years. We divorced a couple of years ago, and since then I've played 2 lines of the same numbers as they do. If they – I mean we – win the jackpot they'll only get a third at most.

RT: 351 FAV: 3,331

Petty Revenge On Husbands and Boyfriends

This is a fat section. Who knew women could be so sneaky?

~~~~

My husband is 51, I'm 48. He really pissed me off the other day, so I signed him up to the Saga mailing list.

RT: 167 FAV: 4,666

I was fed up with my husband not bringing his own reading glasses out with him and always using mine. So I've deliberately bought a pair of bright pink sparkly ones with cat-eye frames. He looks a bit of a twat wearing them in the restaurant, with his shaved head and tatts.

RT: 51 FAV: 4,277

I bought a beautiful 1920s typewriter. My boyfriend hated it, said it was ugly & creepy-looking. I recorded the sound of myself typing on it and hid a Bluetooth speaker in the room, to occasionally secretly play the typing sounds when he's with me. I say I hear nothing.

RT: 235 FAV: 5,820

When watching TV, I often put on the non-HD version of the TV channel, just because I know it will annoy my husband.

RT: 629 FAV: 5,071

I have an open relationship with my bf.
I know when he has other people over to his place when
I see him playing certain songs on his Google speaker
– a speaker linked to my Spotify account. I like to add
boner-killing songs to his queue. 'Baby Shark', usually.

My husband sleeps naked. He does 50 press-ups as
soon as he gets out of bed. I was taking some pics of him
doing them when our cat crept under him and did a big
stretch! I told him I'd deleted the pics but I haven't b/c
I might blackmail him in the future if things go tits up.

My husband has the volume on the TV really
high and plays football podcasts very loudly.
This annoys me, so I deliberately speak to him very
quietly to convince him that he is going deaf .

Men Taking Revenge On Their Women

'Anger is an acid that can do more harm to the vessel in which it is stored than to anything on which it is poured.' Mark Twain

~~~~

My wife regularly has a large and difficult jigsaw on the go. When she goes to bed, I'll solve 3 pieces, then strategically return those to the pile. Next day, when she seems particularly stuck, I walk by nonchalantly solving those pieces. She hates it but it's like a drug for me.

RT: 161 FAV: 3,356

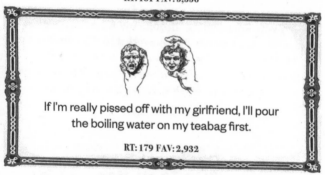

If I'm really pissed off with my girlfriend, I'll pour the boiling water on my teabag first.

RT: 179 FAV: 2,932

When my wife pisses me off, I put her Marmite in the fridge, so that the next day it's hard to spread and fucks up her toast.

RT: 306 FAV: 5,712

If I am slightly annoyed with the wife, when laying the table for dinner I will set the better cutlery at my place. If I am feeling benevolent, I allow her to have what I perceive to be the superior knife and fork.

RT: 91 FAV: 1,651

My wife saw me making tea using unfiltered water. She's convinced she can taste the difference. I've started using filtered water, but every once in a while I sneak in a batch of unfiltered-water tea and she doesn't notice. These are my fave cups because they taste like crime.

RT: 187 FAV: 6,555

My wife and I have a daily Wordle competition and send each other the results. She always does hers first and sends me the results. I know her starting word so can see which letters of STARE are in it – free first guess and I win every time. She thinks I'm some sort of Wordle god.

RT: 171 FAV: 3,500

My wife keeps going through my Amazon account quizzing me on things I've viewed; it really winds me up. So last night I spent an hour viewing pregnancy clothes and newborn products, along with books on extra-marital affairs. Happy Sunday, babe.

RT: 150 FAV: 4,957

Women Fed Up With Their Man

What's got two thumbs and doesn't do the washing-up? A man about to be dumped. Do your share guys, OK?

My husband rarely does the laundry and I'm sick and tired of the imbalance. He ran out of underwear last week and had to resort to wearing swim shorts. He still hasn't put a load of washing on and I'll be damned if I will.

RT: 207 FAV: 4,651

My husband has been arguing with people on the internet for years. Recently I have been able to see some of his posts – and he's not the debating genius he's been claiming he is. At all. I'm quite embarrassed to be married to him now.

RT: 406 FAV: 4,638

My husband has started a football podcast with his friends and thinks he is now a celebrity. It's awful. I cringe every time.

RT: 1,073 FAV: 8,686

Men really annoy me when it comes to pooing. Why can't they just go about their business quietly like women? My boyfriend has to describe the 'absolute scenes' that have just occurred, or say, 'Bigger than King Kong's finger, that.' I don't care.

RT: 499 FAV: 4,364

My husband of 10 years thinks lentils are disgusting. Apparently he hates the texture, the flavour and the look of them. I serve them at least twice a week and he enjoys them a lot. I call them 'beans'.

RT: 371 FAV: 15.4K

I am writing a novel in which the husband is a total prick. He's entirely based on my own husband. My husband doesn't know this. I am confident that when it's published, he won't clock that it's him.

Husband is a dick, turns everything into a battle he has to win. Word games are his bag, including Wordle, which we both do every day. I've never really played it, but simply get the answer online each day to make sure I beat him by at least one turn. It's driving him mental.

My wife has started calling me 'mate'. I fear this could be the beginning of the end of our marriage.

My other half keeps a list on her phone entitled 'Things you shouldn't have to say to a man in his 40s'. It is obviously about me. My favourite entry is: 'Please don't fart in the dishwasher.'

I woke up from a nap the other night to find my bf trying to hide what he was looking at on his phone. After much discussion, he finally showed me: it was a PDF detailing the new font they're using on Ukrainian road signs. I wish it had been porn tbh.

I had a blazing row with my husband about not
storing our new skirting board under our bed,
as it was poking out & causing a trip hazard.
That evening when he tripped over it in the dark
and wrecked himself against the wall was one
of the greatest moments of my life.

Men Fed Up
With Their Women

*One of the reasons for starting Fesshole was to give our friend
Pete somewhere to moan about his wife. Now we're not saying
this section is written by him, but we are saying this is what it
might be like if we published all his DMs.*

~~~~

**My middle-aged wife has started piling on the weight
and wearing dark sunglasses. It's like being married to
Roy Orbison in his twilight years, minus the sideburns.**

Marriage teaches you a lot. Before I got married, I didn't know you could put milk in the fridge the wrong way.

My gf has started doing contouring make-up. She saw it on Insta. I hate it. She looks fine from one specific angle but like she is cosplaying as a tiger from all others.

I'm lying in bed next to my girlfriend. She wants to have sex, but I've just finished a season on *Football Manager* and can't help but lie here and think of ways to improve my team for next season.

When we first started dating, I convinced my girlfriend that farting and belching in front of each other was cute and funny. Now we're married and it's like living with a builder from an 80s sitcom. I hate it.

Both my wife and I have agreed to cremation, when the time comes. She's just told me she wants our ashes mixed. OMG, even when I'm dead, I won't get any peace and quiet.

My wife complains I never buy her flowers anymore, but that's because all that happens afterwards is that I get told to put them in a vase, and then told I've done a shit job arranging them.

I adore my wife, but we didn't live together before we married, and if I'd known that a depressing amount of the evening time we have together would be spent with her watching angry fictional cockneys shout at each other on *EastEnders*, I'd probably not have popped the question.

We have cups with animals on at home. When my girlfriend has been nice, I'll make her tea in the deer cup, because she's been a dear. When she's been a cow, I give her the cow cup. She doesn't know I do this.

RELATIONSHIPS

My girlfriend is cheating on me. I know because
her phone is synced with her iPad, and her messages
pop up when I use it to play *Football Manager*.
I don't really care that she's cheating, I'm just sticking
around until I get sacked on my current save.

RT: 285 FAV: 4,682

**My wife passively aggressively points out my failings
to the dog when I'm in earshot. I tell her this is pathetic,
but when she goes out, I sit him down and give
him my account of events at length.**

RT: 764 FAV: 20.4K

Cheating on Your Partner
Is Never the Answer

*God hates a sinner and will punish them with eternal
damnation for even thinking an impure thought. Actually,
it doesn't work like that, does it? It's just that people cheat,
often get away with it, but have to live with the nagging guilt.*

**I've just arrived at work and one of my colleagues
said he saw me and my wife strolling along the
South Bank having a good time. It wasn't my wife.
I can never bring my wife to social events now.**

RT: 145 FAV: 3,425

I was a serial cheater in my 20s. Since I got married,
I haven't cheated once. I try to tell myself it's because
I'm a better person now, but the truth is, I just got really fat
and bald, and no one's actually interested anymore.

RT: 110 FAV: 2,558

I cheated on my husband, and my dog who never barks started barking and howling at the man. Now any time the man I'm cheating with comes near me, my dog barks. Even my husband has noticed and mentioned it. I can tell she is judging me.

My wife looks through my phone thinking I don't know, but since she became addicted to Wordle, I've started solving it early every day and leaving the result up, so it's the first thing you see when you open the phone... she's stopped looking & I can continue my affair in peace.

Google Street View busted me holding hands with a woman who's not my wife. My face is blurred but it'd be clear to anyone who knows me that it's me. Fortunately it's in a place no one would think to look.

RELATIONSHIPS

'Reader, I Dumped Them'

'DUMP HIM' screams every internet comment on a relationship post. And they're right.

~~~~

Got caught short at my new boyfriend's place but he was in the shower, so I shat in his kitchen bin. I broke up with him while we were out that night just so I wouldn't have to face the music. Sorry Daniel, you were actually quite nice.

RT: 216 FAV: 2,204

After my first-ever one-night stand, the guy I shagged told me his favourite film was *The Iron Lady* and that he idolised Thatcher for 'saving the world'. I haven't stopped scrubbing myself clean ever since.

RT: 571 FAV: 105

A girl I was once seeing introduced me to her kids as 'the TV repairman' because her TV wasn't working properly. I attempted to repair it, made it worse, suffered premature ejaculation and was never contacted again.

RT: 112 FAV: 3,704

I once took a boyfriend to IKEA to instigate an argument so he would break up with me.

RT: 248 FAV: 5,020

I once dumped someone because they didn't like *Paddington 2.*

RT: 605 FAV: 6,855

Dumped my first serious girlfriend using some shit excuse. In reality, when I was doing her from behind, she turned around to look at me & hand on heart I don't know why, but she looked the absolute fucking double of Graham Norton & I couldn't get it out of my mind.

RT: 331 FAV: 2,507

Found my wife having sex on our kitchen sofa at 3am. Kids were asleep upstairs. Pretended to be outraged. Actually I was relieved, as now I can get divorced without guilt.

RT: 378 FAV: 2,927

Tinder date one-night stand. After we shagged a few times I offered to get food. She wanted a walk so we went to the supermarket. She went off and came back with 2 packets of Smash! I then watched in amazement as this fully grown woman ate a saucepan full of instant mashed potato.

RT: 230 FAV: 2,503

My ex-girlfriend used to keep all of her used sanitary products and probably still does. I found this out while I was moving her stuff into my home! She says it's normal; I said it was a deal-breaker and ended the relationship.

RT: 446 FAV: 2,382

RELATIONSHIPS

My worst one-night stand experience as a student was when I went back to a guy's house and when he came he shouted 'Tubby custard!' His housemates all cheered. I ghosted him for that, even though the rest of the date was really good.

RT: 228 FAV: 3,481

People Who Are Trapped in Their Relationship and Can't Get Out

Just *LEAVE!*

I no longer love my girlfriend. But I don't want to leave her 'cos we just got a new sofa that's literally so nice and comfy I don't want anything to come between me and it.

RT: 136 FAV: 2,091

Sometimes when I've had a few beers, I watch my wedding video on rewind. I especially like the bit where they walk backwards down the aisle, get in the car and fuck off into the distance.

RT: 119 FAV: 2,551

Each night I cook my husband a beautiful meal with the plan to tell him that I want to end our marriage. I stop myself each night. I have cooked my way through three Nigel Slater cookbooks so far.

I've completely fallen out of love with my girlfriend, but our friendship group is so tight-knit that I can never break up with her. Her two best friends are dating my two best friends and I love them all so much. I'll probably marry her to keep the gang together.

I'm an aide to a government minister and I can tell you that it's far, far worse than reported. He doesn't even have the most basic grasp of details, everything has to be spoon-fed and it's not some clever front. I should really resign, but I have no skills and huge debts.

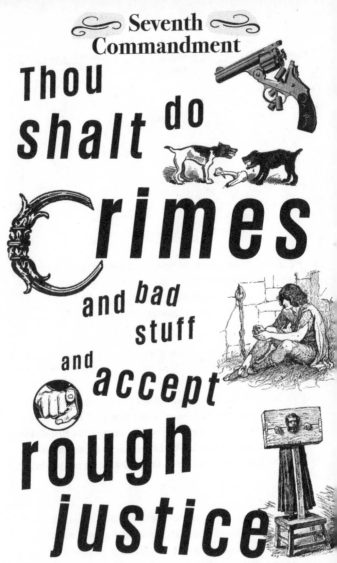

Thou shalt do Crimes and bad stuff and accept rough justice

To the criminal courts of Britain, we submit the following evidence that the entire nation belongs behind bars.

I am a bilingual Brit living in Spain. I regularly translate famous British stand-up comedians' jokes into Spanish and tell them to my Spanish friends. They think I'm hilarious.

RT: 90 FAV: 3,948

I booked a 'man with van' for moving flat. He neglected to turn up on the day. I rang from a friend's number and sent him on an imaginary 120-mile trip to shift some imaginary boxes for an imaginary elderly country gent for an imaginary £300.

RT: 98 FAV: 4,007

The guy I buy weed from voted Tory, so I grassed him up to Crimestoppers. I'll have to find a new dealer but it's worth it.

RT: 231 FAV: 1,634

I had to push my pram into the road this morning because a white Audi had blocked the entire pavement. I keyed the shit out of it. No regrets.

RT: 87 FAV: 1,641

When I worked on the local library, every time we received a new book by Nadine Dorries, I marked it as damaged and threw it straight in the bin. Did the same with David Cameron's autobiography.

RT: 1,310 FAV: 23.3K

When I was about 12, I stole a cheap '110' camera from Boots. I felt guilty so took it to the police station and said I'd found it. One month later, as no one had collected it, the police gave it back to me and said I could keep it.

A fisherman once reversed his truck into my car and refused to pay for the damage. One night when the tide was out I walked out to his boat, untied it and watched the tide come in and his boat float away.

In John Lewis car park in Kingston upon Thames, someone parked so close to my driver's side that I had to get my son into his baby seat from the wrong side then crawl over myself. With a 50p, I left a deep gouge all along the side of the other car.

I got made redundant by a total arsewipe of a company and when I left, I had to hand back my Apple Mac. Three years later, I remotely wiped the whole damned unit and I don't feel a bit guilty.

So I think I've been challenged to a fist fight. I'm 57. It's a no-lose proposition for me. The story is either 'young man assaults a borderline pensioner' or 'old bloke kicks some punk's arse'.

Thou Shalt Do Crimes.
Bad-Ass Crimes.

~~~~~~

All of these people have got a tattoo saying
'Baddest motherfucker in Tunbridge Wells'.

~~~~

When I'm dragged kicking and screaming to IKEA, I make it my
mission to pocket as many free small pencils and measuring
tapes as possible. My record is 58 pencils and 22 tapes.

RT: 101 FAV: 2,138

**When I was 15, I stole two paperback books from a local
bookstore. I knew the proprietor wouldn't know, because
he was blind. It's haunted me my whole adult life. Now
I give money every year to charities for the blind.**

RT: 84 FAV: 3,640

I once found a wallet. It was nicer than mine,
so I just swapped the contents of my wallet and
theirs and handed it in. I still crack up thinking about
the guy going to the police station and being like,
'That's not my wallet,' and then seeing all of his stuff in it.

RT: 322 FAV: 3,212

**At a restaurant, me & my friend noticed that a couple
had left a lot of their shared pizza. We decided to eat
their 'leftovers', only to be told by the waiter that the
couple had only gone out for a cigarette. Managed to pay
up before the couple returned to a clean plate.**

RT: 211 FAV: 4,018

I buy trolley tokens for 35p from Home Bargains and when I'm at the supermarket and have loaded up the car, I spot someone about to get a trolley and offer mine and take their pound coin.

RT: 283 FAV: 3,630

I stay in hotels in and around London for work. When getting a pint after a day's graft, I have one rule: if the pint costs more than £6, I am stealing the glass for my bar at home. If you're robbing me, then I'm robbing you back.

RT: 433 FAV: 101

Graduated from university 3 years ago. For some reason my .ac.uk email address has not been closed down yet. Still reaping all the student discount benefits. Not sorry at all.

RT: 25 FAV: 2,085

I worked in a CD manufacturing plant in the hols. Mostly total music crap but the 2nd Oasis CD – *What's the Story* – came in to be printed before release. I smuggled the master copy out in my pants, copied it on to cassette and all my friends got pre-release copies. I was a hero.

RT: 63 FAV: 3,937

I bought a second-hand PS4 from eBay for £50. The previous owner hadn't wiped his account, so now I get free Sky, BT Sport and Netflix. Thanks eBay account G@ryStar1977.

RT: 121 FAV: 6,768

Once read how spies set up false IDs in case they need to disappear. I tried it and it worked. I have an alter ego that I maintain, complete with birth certificate, passport etc, just in case. I'm 45 and work in a call centre.

As a teenager, I illegally downloaded over 10,000 albums. I now work in the music industry but I'm still not sorry. I'm certain I never would have developed my passion if I only had the 2 or 3 CDs a year I could afford with my pocket money.

At 16/17, I was very drunk walking home from a house party at 2am when I saw some guys moving, so I ended up helping them carry a TV + speakers etc out to a car. When I sobered up & told a friend about my good deed, I realised I had probably helped them rob a house. Who moves at 2am?

'I Only Read Fesshole for the Shoplifting Tips'

Petty theft is endemic in the UK and apparently we've been encouraging it. Please don't shoplift this book, although if you do, send us a confession about it, OK?

~~~~

I had massive tits in my pregnancy and found I could quickly shoplift a large bar of Cadbury's Dairy Milk under each boob if I didn't wear a bra.

I found the Greggs coffee stamp on eBay for £20.
I've not paid for a coffee from Greggs in over 2 years.

**I don't pay for any birthday cards, I just slip
them into a weekend newspaper and run it
through the self-checkout. As there is no set weight
for the newspaper, it can't detect the increase.
I'm not paying £2.50 for a bit of folded card.**

When doing the food shop, I bundle two packs of
spring onions together and remove one of the tags to
get more for my money. Every little helps.

**I frequently make money back by 'refunding' used
train tickets that haven't been scanned or punched.
It's saved me £100s over the years. I used to feel guilty
but the last few years of politics and privatisation
means I don't give a shit.**

Several years back, I photocopied my Clubcard barcode, printed it on a self-adhesive label and stuck it over my colleague's card. He collected Clubcard points for me for about 12 months. We no longer work together and haven't spoken since.

RT: 91 FAV: 2,885

Worked at Morrisons when I was 18. I'd get 5 or 6 family friends to come and do their big shop on a Saturday and not scan the expensive stuff like meat and booze. Save them each about £60 a shop then go and collect £20 each off all of them ready for a Saturday night on the piss.

RT: 282 FAV: 5,115

As a former Tesco till worker, I used to reprint all receipts where a customer didn't use their Clubcard and load the potential points on to mine. I was racking up an easy £10 each week and it's amazing I never got caught.

RT: 205 FAV: 5,694

Bought an Apple Watch and had it delivered to a parcel pick-up spot in Matalan. They scanned it wrong and it was never marked as collected. They tried calling several times and I ignored it. Apple refunded my order as it ended up being marked 'lost'. I have the Apple Watch. Result.

RT: 58 FAV: 2,918

Got caught sneaking into the Man Utd exec lounge with free food & booze. They took the lanyard I used to bypass security, claiming they have CCTV footage of me stealing it. Truth is, I bought it off eBay for £5, I've snuck in all season and have three extra lanyards at home.

RT: 203 FAV: 6,218

People Who Might Actually Go to Jail if We Share Their IP Addresses With the Feds

People often ask us if Fesshole is just one large blackmail plot where we get the confessions and then tap them for cash. It's all true and these are the people paying our mortgage.

~~~~

I faked my ex-husband's signature on our divorce papers. Couldn't find the fat twat and wanted to get rid of him.

RT: 266 FAV: 9,574

Friend and I got coke while in Edinburgh for the weekend. Were flying home so couldn't take it back with us. Posted it to myself in a birthday card. Quite proud of my genius, but can't tell anyone.

RT: 145 FAV: 3,762

Worked in the strong room – money-counting secure area – at a UK theme park with a load of teenagers counting money all day. The thievery was rife. One day the loo stopped flushing. I opened the lid and found £1,500 in damp notes. Nicked it, bought a car. No regrets.

RT: 26 FAV: 2,638

When part-exing my car, the online trade-in price was £200 less for not having both keys. Bought a £9 key fob off Amazon and slotted it in to the clear folder with the log & service book. They noted that it was present when collecting the car but didn't bother to check if it worked.

I was once in a bar and on the counter they had picture frames full of counterfeit notes to show they couldn't be fooled by them. Anyway, we robbed both of the frames, smashed them and paid the £60 taxi home using the demonstrative fake £20s.

As a teen living at home, I'd pay my parents £250 per month board. They didn't need the money but wanted to teach me the value of it. I was skint one month, so I changed my direct debit payment to them to £2.50 just in case they scanned through their statements. It worked.

When I cook a ready meal, I don't stir it halfway through its cooking time as per the instructions.

CRIME

I Miss Drugs

Drugs generally get put away as people age and become parents and/or responsible adults, but isn't there still part of you that wants to get some mushrooms and wander about the local woods looking for gnomes?

~~~~

Bored with my mid-30s boring middle-class life, whenever I open a bottle of red wine, I stamp the cork on my wrist and reminisce about the days I used to go clubbing.

RT: 127 FAV: 4,473

Just listening to some early 90s techno and realising that, as a 51-year-old guy, I'm never again going to experience anything even close to the absolute pure unadulterated joy of coming up on some really good pills in a sweaty club and dancing till 8am. Nothing comes close.

RT: 352 FAV: 3,116

I'm a carpenter. When tidying up at work, I like to rack up the sawdust into lines and make Henry hoover snort it up like the dirty junkie he is.

RT: 164 FAV: 1,898

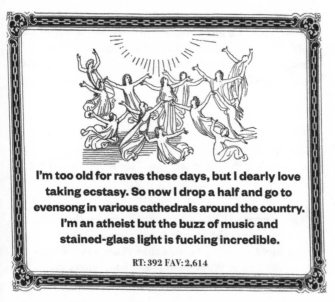

I'm too old for raves these days, but I dearly love taking ecstasy. So now I drop a half and go to evensong in various cathedrals around the country. I'm an atheist but the buzz of music and stained-glass light is fucking incredible.

RT: 392 FAV: 2,614

I am a teacher and mother of two. I'm usually very risk-averse and sensible. But, when I listen to *Leftism* by Leftfield, I drive like an amphetamine- and LSD-fuelled 16-year-old. I crashed into a tractor this morning on the way back from the school run.

RT: 131 FAV: 1,988

I called Radio 1 at 3 in the morning while on acid to ask them how to make apple crumble.

RT: 180 FAV: 2,509

Me and my best mate spent the weekend of 30th August 1997 smoking weed and doing magic mushrooms and LSD. We saw a newspaper headline on Monday that Princess Diana had died and freaked out because we thought we'd been high/tripping for 50 years and she'd died of old age.

RT: 215 FAV: 6,920

After going to a rave in the 90s, me and my mate got invited back to a girl's house. We were on for a sure thing with her and her mate until they caught me in the dog basket licking their Dalmatian, thinking it was a giant humbug. They asked us to leave. Don't do drugs, kids.

Around 18 years ago, I took a load of ecstasy in the house alone and woke up to discover I'd changed all the contacts in my phone to the name 'Jeff'. Took me weeks to sort out.

I got arrested while on ecstasy. I was really horny, so in my cell I had a 4-hour wank sitting against the door so they couldn't see me through the hatch. When being released, I saw the screen with all the different cell cameras.

Fighting Capitalism
One Step at a Time

We all want capitalism to fall and for it to be replaced by a high-tech socialist utopia, and these are the good people doing their bit to destroy the machine from within.

I have a Tesco credit card. I make one purchase per month and pay it in full, minus 99p. Then on my next statement, they always scrap the 99p as a small balance write-off. I like to think of it as a small victory for the common man. £5.99 worth of goods for a fiver? Yes please!

Amazon don't pay their taxes. So I order stuff and say I haven't received it. Fuck you, Amazon.

Got a call from a random number. A guy was telling me he was late for work. He must have thought I was his boss. So I gave him the day off. He even texted and asked if I was sure. I said, 'Yeah, don't worry.' But he sounded happy as Larry when I got off the phone with him!

Every time I take a flight somewhere, I tell the airline that I have a severe peanut allergy, just so they can't sell them and miss out on the ridiculous profits they make. It's the little things.

I got a temp job in an office but due to some crossed wires was given literally no actual work to do. I decided against pointing this out to anyone and instead made myself look busy every day for four months by becoming an absolutely prolific Wikipedia editor.

In the 90s when Wash & Go was launched in the UK, free samples were supposed to get delivered with the post. Let's just say this postman still has great hair and will do for many years to come. Sorry P&G.

RT: 24 FAV: 1,733

I worked for years for Royal Mail. As posties, we got paid extra to deliver 'door-to-door' mail – junk mail to everyone else. I took most of it home and burnt it. I was never caught and pocketed the money. Fuck you, capitalism.

RT: 39 FAV: 1,825

Getting One Over on the Middle Classes

~~~~~~

The middle class is a group of people in the middle of society, between the upper and lower classes. They are usually well-educated and have good jobs. And they're an easy mark for a wily commoner.

~~~~

I'm a professional decorator. Whenever posh middle-aged women demand I use a certain paint brand, I colour-match it at B&Q and then invoice them for the price of the branded stuff. None of them has ever had the sense to ask to see receipts. Not remotely sorry.

RT: 727 FAV: 10.5K

I'm a builder. 15 years ago I found £40k in a house I was renovating that belonged to the previous owner. I pocketed the lot rather than tell the new owners, who went on to tell their friends how generous I was for not charging for small odd jobs I did for them afterwards.

RT: 151 FAV: 4,586

Whenever I find myself passing through a quaint Cotswold village, I make sure to tell the proprietor of the local newsagent that I just saw a fleet of travellers' caravans heading their way. The look of alarm and panic on the locals' smug middle-class faces quite cheers me up.

RT: 231 FAV: 5,079

I like to occasionally swap eggs from the fancy Burford Brown box for the cheap-as-chips eggs in the shop. I like to imagine some pompous twat going on about how nice the eggs taste.

RT: 54 FAV: 3,432

As a student, I worked in a very high-end boutique, and was sometimes acting manager on Saturdays. Once I bought a pair of £15 stilettos from Primark, destickered them and put them on our middle-of-store plinth, priced £480. Sold them by lunchtime – buyer paid cash.

RT: 497 FAV: 13.1K

When attending a customer's home as a tradesman, I'll often hand them a five-pound note as they answer the door and claim it must belong to them as I found it on the path. The instant trust this creates makes it a lot easier to overcharge them later on.

RT: 866 FAV: 14

Taking the Law Into Their Own Hands

Imagine if the police were just some random people deciding what should or shouldn't happen. Wouldn't that be fun?

~~~~

Saw a bloke obviously drunk-driving on a dual carriageway. Stayed behind. He came off at my junction and pulled over for a piss. Doubled back. He was still pissing, so I took his keys – still in ignition – and lobbed them as far as I could into a field. Shopped him to the police.

RT: 258 FAV: 8,465

When my grandma moved house, she stole her old neighbour's dog. The dog had spent its life chained up to a kennel in a muddy garden. Authorities said no laws were being broken as the dog had shelter and water. Grandma decided that was a shit answer. Dog lived a great life with her.

RT: 341 FAV: 6,834

If I'm making a cup of tea for someone and they ask for sugar, I use a third less sugar than requested. They shouldn't be having sugar in their tea as adults.

RT: 962 FAV: 9,917

I stole a £40 tin of paint from B&Q. Painted my living room in it; didn't like it, so gave it a bad review on their website.

RT: 145 FAV: 2,404

I have a small car. In busy car parks, I like to park it between two big cars so it's hidden away and makes other drivers think there's an empty space until they get near enough to park in it.

The Almighty Injustice of Helping to Save a Life and Not Getting a Thank You

~~~~~~

Hopefully appearing in this weighty tome is a belated thank you to these heroes.

~~~~

I witnessed a bad car accident & gave CPR to the driver. Brought him back to life and once the ambulance arrived, they took over. I put his girlfriend in my car and put my hoodie on her. She didn't return the hoodie & bled all over my fucking seat. Never heard a word of thanks. Fuming.

A few years ago, I anonymously donated my bone marrow, presumably to someone who would have died without it. Not even a card to let me know if they're alive or dead. Fucking fuming.

Five years ago I saved a boy's life in a Norwich park when he wandered off & fell in a pond. I jumped in, saved him & magnanimously left once he was safe. There was no news article, no 'Who was the mysterious hero?' FB appeal, nothing. I've been fucking furious about it ever since.

But God Rewards a Cheat

~~~~~~

*It's a horrible life lesson, but the people who get ahead
in life cheat. Well, not all of them, but a lot of them. Look at our
current crop of politicians. (This line will never date, whoever
is in power, as most people will be grumpy about them.)*

~~~~

**I once had a temp job in university admin, printing
degree certificates. On my last day, I printed myself a
certificate with the award of MA in Interpretive Dance.**

RT: 197 FAV: 8,094

A lady just made her toddler son sit on his dad's lap so I could
have a seat on a crowded train. She thought I was pregnant.
I am in fact just fat and hungover, and you bet I took that seat.

RT: 77 FAV: 5,143

**While at uni on a teaching degree, I had to submit a
computing assignment on a CD. There were over 250
students and I figured they wouldn't look at everyone's
so I submitted a blank CD. I got 63%. It reinforced my
view that it's better to work smarter, not harder.**

RT: 130 FAV: 5,459

My quiz team recently won, it was a cash prize. The other members used their phones to cheat. I felt so guilty about it that I donated my winnings to a mental health charity.

RT: 34 FAV: 3,149

The poem that got me an A in GCSE English was actually the lyrics to 'Father to Son' by Queen. I figured no one would know it and I was right. Thanks, Freddie.

RT: 242 FAV: 5,259

Worked a summer job at a store where you could win 10 kilos of candy & a stay at a resort if you could guess the correct number of marbles in a jar. While working the night shift, me and my colleague counted the marbles and submitted the answer via our parents. Both won 1st prize.

RT: 36 FAV: 2,735

A local farm charges £100 for a family ticket. They ran a drawing competition with a family ticket as the prize. I drew a bunny with my left hand and entered as my 18-month-old daughter. Won the ticket. Not sorry.

RT: 92 FAV: 4,914

My husband started an Open University degree last year. He asked me to check his essay. Turns out he can't think critically or write sentences. 6 months later, he's on track for a 1st. Bless him, he doesn't even get that this is cheating.

RT: 197 FAV: 6,628

I lied about my qualifications in an interview for a well-paid job. Shortly after I joined, my new boss died suddenly, so when HR asked for proof of qualifications, I told them I'd given all the original copies to him. I heard no more about it. It's been 3 years and I still live in fear.

At school, we were asked to write down the name of someone we'd lost. I hadn't lost anyone, so I put down Roz Forrester from the Dr Who *New Adventures* – Adric would've been weird. Later that day we had a Mass in our church, and the priest read out the whole list.

More Petty Revenge

~~~~~~

Revenge is sweetest when it's petty and out of all proportion.

~~~~

Got into a heated debate on Twitter about politics. I looked at the guy's profile and noticed he was right into Wordle. I played that day's game just after midnight, then messaged him the spoiler. Hopefully made his day a bit worse.

I work in one of London's best five-star hotels, which happens to be in Westminster. We get lots of Tories in for tea/coffee. I always make sure it's too hot to drink or so weak it's pointless. It's a little victory I have that won't result in me being sacked.

Met a disgusting racist on a hen party, which happened to be on a cruise around Sydney Harbour. She spent half of the cruise looking for her $1,000 Prada handbag, which is now lying at the bottom of Sydney Harbour. Whoops.

RT: 381 FAV: 148

I'm pretty good at online video games, and while playing I get my kid sister to speak for me and bad-mouth the other players. It drives the nerds fucking mental, thinking they are being beaten by a small girl.

RT: 255 FAV: 3,314

Someone rammed their trolley into my ankle at Tesco and it hurt. They didn't apologise, so I followed them until they walked away from their trolley, and I picked up their self-scan scanner and scanned extra stuff so they would have had to pay for items they didn't pick up.

RT: 146 FAV: 4,069

Someone was standing way too close behind me in Greggs just now, ignoring not only social distancing but just plain old personal space. Overheard her order before she placed it, so I had the last two sausage rolls she wanted.

RT: 169 FAV: 6,935

People in the next hotel room partied noisily till nearly 3. We had an early start, so I phoned their room with the 'early morning call' they'd 'requested' at 6 when I got up for a shower, 6.30 when we went for breakfast, 7 when we returned and 7.30 when we left.

RT: 59 FAV: 2,270

I really don't like a guy at work. To mildly inconvenience him, sometimes when I go into work I try to log in using his name and a few random passwords. It locks his PC for an hour every morning.

RT: 288 FAV: 7,037

Two tradesmen got into their van and proceeded to throw their Greggs rubbish out of the window. That night, I spent three hours writing bad reviews about their business on as many review sites as I could find.

RT: 339 FAV: 109

I like to use the prepaid envelopes from junk mail to send the company other 'interesting' mail I receive. I have just sent a Screwfix catalogue to a PPI claim company.

RT: 911 FAV: 16.3K

Found some car keys on the street. Walked round the area pressing unlock on the off-chance of finding the right car & returning them. Opened a car parked on a drive. Was about to hand the keys in when I noticed a 'Britain First' sticker in their window. Dumped them in a bin instead.

RT: 575 FAV: 143

Thou shalt experience Regret

These people have experienced regret.
And not in that one good New Order single way.

I read in Jason Manford's autobiography about him walking out of his telesales job and how it was the best feeling. I decided to do the same in January and felt nothing but dread and fear. I am currently 3 months unemployed and skint.

When I was 18, I worked for a watch company in London. I had to deliver a Rolex to a beautiful woman at Heathrow, who was surprising her bf with it and a holiday. She got stood up and asked me if I wanted to go. It haunts me to this day that I didn't go, 30 years later.

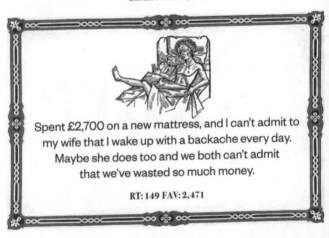

Spent £2,700 on a new mattress, and I can't admit to my wife that I wake up with a backache every day. Maybe she does too and we both can't admit that we've wasted so much money.

On the beach, I needed a huge shit. Headed to the sand dunes and did my business. I cleaned myself up and was about to scarper when a German Shepherd bounded over the dunes, followed by an old man who picked up my shit with his gloved hand and apologised to me profusely. Haunts me.

I accidentally pulled the emergency cord in the disabled loo at work. Panicked, I ran to the other toilet. When I came out, I joined in the search to try and find the disabled individual to see if they were OK, never admitting it was me.

RT: 55 FAV: 2,769

I Look Back and Cringe So Hard

Do you ever find yourself stopping dead, in the middle of washing-up, remembering something stupid you did 20 years ago? Welcome to the cringe zone.

~~~~

I once shared a table in a pub with Kelly Jones of Stereophonics. After too much wine, I told him I hadn't enjoyed his performance at V Festival & gave him some tips on how he could improve things. I'm a civil servant, and can't sing or play instruments. I've been cringing for 12 years.

RT: 236 FAV: 1,270

Sat next to a beautiful girl on a long-distance train journey. After an hour or so, I needed the toilet and wanted to ask politely if I could 'squeeze out'. What I actually said was, 'I need to squeeze one out.' She had moved by the time I came back.

RT: 173 FAV: 6,330

New to social media and WhatsApp a few years back, I sent my wife my very first dick pic. 15 seconds later, I realised to my horror I'd attached it to 'family group'. I deleted the app the following day. We have never spoken of it, but they all know of my shame.

RT: 46 FAV: 2,029

When with my girlfriend, I always make an orgasm moan when plugging in an aux cable, as it always makes her laugh. I plugged in my headphones on the train today and did my sex moan without thinking in front of a little old lady. Spent the rest of the journey in the loo.

RT: 85 FAV: 4,948

Wife sent picture of her milking a goat on family WhatsApp group. Replied 'Can't wait for you to milk me like that later' to the group chat rather than to her. I didn't realise. My mum, dad, brother and sister-in-law are all in the group. Ah well.

RT: 138 FAV: 527

When I was saying bye to a guy I'd just slept with, I patted his willy and said thank you. I have no idea why, and I self-implode with cringe every time I think about it.

RT: 368 FAV: 6,331

Our pizza was 40 minutes late so I called the pizza place. They had no record of our order. I insisted they look and they went to get the manager. Our pizza then arrived – from a different pizza place. I just hung up the phone. Mortified.

RT: 60 FAV: 2,673

When I was young and exceptionally clueless, I paid a cheer-up visit to a colleague in hospital. In the labour ward. While she was in labour. Astonishingly, she did not want to see me. I have no idea why I thought this was in any way socially appropriate. It still makes me cringe.

RT: 80 FAV: 2,048

Raging, I returned my new £400 pram to John Lewis because it broke within a month. The staff were polite and apologetic and loaned me a replacement and said they'd fix it within 48 hours. Husband rang and I told him what happened. He said 'But we got it from Mothercare...'

RT: 289 FAV: 8,453

Wandering round the supermarket, I found an Asda employee and asked her where the eggs were. She led me round the shop to point them out and as I turned to thank her, I realised I was in Lidl and she was just doing her shopping.

RT: 268 FAV: 7,740

Went for an interview in a steakhouse. It went OK until the owner, who was there during the interview, asked 'What do you know about me?' I said, 'Absolutely nothing.' He laughed, thanked me, and I left. On the walk home, I realised he'd asked 'What do you know about meat?'

RT: 178 FAV: 3,671

My wife bought a dash cam for our car. I didn't know it recorded the sound in the car. She now has lots of recordings of me pretending to be interviewed by Sky Sports as manager of my *FIFA* team while driving to work. Mortifying.

RT: 2,818 FAV: 55.5K

I've Got a Secret That I Can Never Tell

~~~~~~

Our secret that we can never share is that we're addicted to tractor porn. Note for the publisher: please make sure that this doesn't get printed in 10,000 copies, thank you.

~~~~

When I was a kid, I used to swap the batteries out of my mum's vibrator with my Game Boy Color batteries when they ran out so I could keep playing Pokémon Blue.

RT: 160 FAV: 1,793

Wife left her car lights on & got a simple flat battery. I cocked up a jump start, blew all the fuses & destroyed the starter motor. It's cost nearly £1k to fix. I've not admitted I did the real damage & she thinks it's her fault. We've had to skip this year's holiday.

RT: 85 FAV: 2,185

I met my husband before we had mobile phones, which is lucky because if we'd been texting when dating, I'd have dumped him for his shit spelling and complete lack of knowledge on which their, there or they're to use.

RT: 290 FAV: 7,722

My wife and I have been struggling for 8 years to have a baby. On my birthday, my wife asked me to make a wish as I blew out the candles on my cake. I did. I wished for Arsenal to finish 4th so we can buy a world-class striker in the summer.

RT: 789 FAV: 7,420

In films, they show prostitutes being paid afterwards. That's not how it works. The john always pays up front. It annoys me every time, but I just can't say anything when we're watching as a family.

RT: 173 FAV: 3,625

My wife always complains that our 18-month-old son doesn't look anything like her – he doesn't – so I set him up a Face ID on her phone to stop her moaning. Every time he unlocks her phone, it brings her so much joy. I will never tell her.

RT: 120 FAV: 5,035

My child's teacher set maths homework on the school website to answer 20 easy questions. Wife had a go using the lad's log-in and bossed it. A month later, he won an award for being in the top 10 in the world. Turns out it was an international competition.

RT: 131 FAV: 3,089

We have courtesy umbrellas at work and I emptied a vast load of paper hole punches into one as a prank. Forgot about it, and this week a VIP used one with the CEO when going for lunch. Big investigation ongoing. I'm keeping very quiet.

My wife and I had a ding-dong sexy session in the kitchen. A cucumber was used and it was a jolly good time. What wasn't a good time was seven o'clock in the morning when our six-year-old woke us up while eating it. She's 19 now and I will never tell her.

If somebody ever hacks my laptop and releases my private browsing history, the most embarrassing bit won't be the porn, it'll be all the times I have to google words that I really should know how to spell by now.

My husband made me orgasm through penetrative sex for the first time last night. I was thrilled! But couldn't share my joy with him 'cos he thinks he's been doing it for the last 15 years.

A mate got in touch promoting their band's new song. I clicked the link and listened, blown away by how good it was, and sent him a gushing text. When I went to play it to my wife, I realised that I had accidentally listened to 'Dreams' by Fleetwood Mac. His actual song is shit.

People Who Are
Quite Possibly Going to Hell

*Confessing at the Church of Fesshole might not always result
in forgiveness. Can you forgive these people?*

~~~~

**My mum had trouble sleeping, so before I went
home, I crumbled some hash into her coffee thinking
it would help. 2 hours later, I had to return &
tell paramedics what I'd done as she freaked
out and called 999. Sorry, Mum.**

RT: 83 FAV: 2,666

Made shroom tea at home then went out tripping for a few
hours. Came home to find Mum under the bedsheets claiming
a man with a knife was trying to kill her. House was empty.
Then I realised I'd forgotten to empty and rinse out the teapot.
Still haven't told her 30 years later.

RT: 146 FAV: 3,819

**I was in a rough area of town and saw a homeless
person standing outside a store with a coffee cup
with no lid. I stopped, put my spare change in and
was horrified when it made a 'glunk' sound.
I had just put coins into a person's drink.**

RT: 90 FAV: 2,289

I had to sack someone on the spot for gross misconduct.
She cried. That night, I was telling my wife about my day
& then we got on to topic of what to eat. I said I was full,
there had been a lot of cake in the office that day.
Then I realised – I'd sacked the girl on her birthday.

**Mate was gutted when he found out his long-term
girlfriend was shagging a bloke from her work.
As retribution, we all took turns shitting in a bin liner for
a week, then one night we threw it all over the front of
what turned out to be some other poor cunt's house.**

Walking home from a night out, I spotted a paper cup on
the pavement begging to be volleyed into an imaginary top
corner. It wasn't until the coins went flying down the road
that I turned & saw the homeless man whose day's donations
were now strewn in the gutter. I'm going to hell.

**Postman here. I saw a cat trying to get into a window
so helped him in and pushed the window closed.
Two weeks later, homeowners came back from
holiday to a load of shit everywhere and a dead cat.
It wasn't their cat. Sorry.**

Dressed up as Fred West for Halloween one year.
Was going well until I was mistaken for Tom Jones by a
group of OAPs in the pub. Ended up singing 'It's Not Unusual'
to a bar full of very confused zombies.

Once needed a day off work, so told my manager my gran had died. Took 3 days off work and when I returned, to my horror, colleagues had done a collection, signed a card and bought a bunch of flowers for my nan. I spent the collection money on a night out. I'm going to hell.

Just gave the middle finger to a big group holding anti-vax placards on the Tyne Bridge. Turns out they were anti-war placards and I'm a proper dick.

Last winter my granddaughter, who is registered blind, was staying with us for 10 days. In the run-up to Christmas, she was getting increasingly bored and I was out of ideas. At my wits' end, I got her to wrap presents. Including her own presents.

Thou Shalt Feel Guilty, It's the Catholic Way

Guilt is a fantastic emotion to help you behave better. Avoid those horrible feelings by not doing anything terrible. Well, unless you're a psychopath – then all bets are off.

Desperately wanting to beat my brother in a charity treasure hunt, I cheated slightly. Unbeknown to me, so did he. We won 1st & 2nd prizes. Overwhelmed with guilt, we donated our prize monies back to the charity, only to be then held up as the most decent and generous people ever.

**My dog is getting old and he can only
manage short walks. I take him for a short walk
and then sneak out later for a longer walk.
He probably knows. I feel such a rat.**

RT: 106 FAV: 2,982

I gave a homeless guy £20 one winter's day. I found out the
next day he had overdosed during the night. I have been
riddled with guilt that I facilitated his death.

RT: 272 FAV: 2,569

**In the 1990s, I engaged in transactions with a sex worker
4 times. She was in the news 3 weeks after our last
meeting, found murdered. I was terrified I'd be a suspect.
Couldn't tell my wife why I was stressed. Thankfully they
caught the bloke quite quick. Never cheated again.**

RT: 191 FAV: 3,289

I met a girl on a night out, went back to her place & fucked.
When we finished, she broke down & told me she had cancer.
Told her I was going the toilet but lied & ran home.
I felt guilty, often wondering if she had died, then a few
years later I saw her at train station – she made it.

RT: 258 FAV: 4,897

Naughty Liars Who Need a Good Spanking

~~~~~~

Lying is not a sin, getting caught lying is.

When I was a teenager, I pretended to be scared of squirrels to seem quirky and different. 25 years down the line, and I still have to pretend to be scared of them 'cos I've maintained friendships from high school. I'm not remotely afraid of squirrels. Even my husband thinks I am.

RT: 3 FAV: 1,430

I took a photo of a waterfall near Perth in Scotland and labelled it 'Waterfall by Aberystwyth'. I sent it to a competition run by the Welsh tourist board and won second prize. It was the February photo in the 'Best pictures of Wales' calendar that year.

RT: 236 FAV: 9,936

Lied on a date about having a Harley Davidson to sound edgy & secure sex. 3 months, it in got serious, so I had to get motorbike licence & spend my inheritance on an overpriced motorbike I look like a twat riding.

RT: 286 FAV: 6,096

When I first met my girlfriend, I told her I was an orphan to get a sympathy shag. It worked and we've been together for 6 months. My mum really wants to meet her now.

To fill a gap in my CV, I've said that I was a guitarist for The Fall for a brief period. No one has disputed this or even asked questions about it.

I Wanted the Ground to Swallow Me Up

Please dig us a hole so we can climb in with these poor people and never speak to a human being again.

In TK Maxx, I saw a jumper discarded over the top of a rail of clothes. I liked it but couldn't see a price tag. As I pulled it over my head to try it on, a wallet fell on to the floor. I picked it up and handed it to the guy staring at me. He asked if he could have his jumper back too.

At primary school, the teacher told us it was the Christmas party the next day and so to all come to school 'dressed up'. The following day everyone turned up in smart clothes, and I turned up as a red Indian with full headdress and tomahawk.

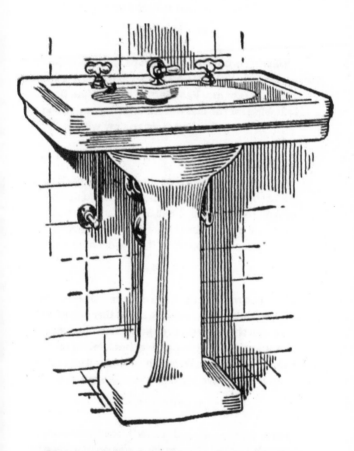

My daughter caught me pissing in the bathroom sink. 15 years of near-perfect parenting and this is what she'll remember.

RT: 73 FAV: 4,485

Upon noticing a change of surname, I congratulated
my colleague on her recent marriage.
Turns out she'd just got divorced.

**Walking around clothes shops with the wife,
it was cold outside and I had chapped lips, so I asked her
'Have you got any Vaseline?' The girl I had been
following for the last few minutes turned round
looking shocked. It wasn't my wife.**

I once reported to HR that one of my staff needed
extra support due to being possibly suicidal as he
had a permanent note to 'call Samaritans' in his diary.
Turns out he did house clearances on the side and
had to book to drop off stuff at the charity shop.

**I pissed on my wife during a drunken sleep-walk.
Our son woke at the noise & came through when
she was showering. I drunkenly told him what
happened while tucking him back in. He told
his teacher because I'd said he could tell a teacher
anything. Gave parents evening a swerve.**

Walked up to my wife and started holding her hand in
Sainsbury's. I looked at her to find a woman I'd never seen
before looking amazed/horrified, and then saw my wife
pissing herself laughing at me. I'm still mortified 5 years
later and my wife still takes the piss for it.

Said the Wrong Thing

Have you ever said the wrong thing?
Maybe you've called your history teacher 'mum' like we did.

~~~~

I once went to a pizza restaurant and the waitress asked if I'd like my pizza cut into 4 or 8 slices. I replied 4 'cos I wasn't sure I could eat 8. Pretty sure that's the dumbest thing I've ever said.

RT: 240 FAV: 5,583

Whenever people ask me to guess their age, I always take 5 years of my initial thought so I flatter and don't offend. When asked today by a colleague, I said 'Ohh, I don't know, 55!' She replied 'Ohh close, 53.'

RT: 145 FAV: 3,866

I accidentally said 'happy birthday' instead of 'hello' at the start of an interview over Zoom and pretended I was talking to my cat. I didn't get the job.

RT: 127 FAV: 2,727

In my early twenties, having never ordered steak before, when asked how I wanted it cooked, I answered 'In an oven?'

RT: 447 FAV: 2,860

I was chatting to a colleague after starting a new job. 'Have you met Nathan?' she asked. I said yes and described him as a 'likeable idiot' who 'I wouldn't trust to tie his own shoelaces'. Conversation over; Nathan was her son.

One of my friends attends the same gym as me. I saw him in the changing room naked, so I walked towards him pointing at his genitals and said, 'Most have them in adult size.' It was at this moment I realised it wasn't him. I now need a new gym.

During lockdown, I went for a park date with a woman and her dog. I embraced the dog and said 'hello sexy' instead of 'hello gorgeous'. It was a very quiet walk.

I am Revolting and I'm Sorry (Not Sorry)

~~~~~~

This is the piss and shit material, so hold your nose, OK?

~~~~

On a 1st date, a lovely stroll around the river with a girl and her Boxer. I needed the toilet so bad that I let her dog off the leash, sprinted after it, quickly dropped trou and did a poo while out of sight. Then I blamed it on her dog. I watched her pick it up after.

I got on the bus and it stunk of piss. I was disgusted, told everyone at work about how bad the buses are getting. The next day it happened again. I was looking round, thinking, who is the dirty smelly bastard? On the 3rd day, I realised my dog had pissed on my jacket.

RT: 93 FAV: 5,424

Got caught short in the shower. Rather than hop out and get the toilet wet, I squatted and cupped my hands underneath my asshole followed by a severely concentrated under-arm throw across the bathroom. Boom, nailed it.

RT: 301 FAV: 1,399

Quite drunk and needing a piss, I went to the toilet in the club. Fuck knows how I did this, but I unzipped and pulled out my left bollock thinking I had got my dick and pissed myself.

RT: 376 FAV: 7,603

Back in the summer, I was trimming my pubes in the bathroom and decided to throw the trimmings out of the window, as the wife usually complains about the mess of hairs everywhere. Seconds later, I heard screams from the neighbours as the wind blew hairs into their alfresco dining.

RT: 464 FAV: 2,305

I deep-cleaned the bathroom today, and put the bog brush and toilet plunger through the dishwasher to get them super clean. No poo present, came out sparkly clean. The wife still went mental. Still not sure why I haven't earned man points for this.

RT: 289 FAV: 2,259

I once shat my pants on a school camping trip and disposed of said soiled pants in another boy's wellington boot. A day or so later, the heavens opened and we were told to don our wellies. I'll never forget the loud scream heard over the camp when he put his foot in that Dunlop.

On a Japan Airlines flight, I drank 3 cups of sake followed by a Stilnox sleeping tablet. I woke up after a long sleep feeling terrible, and the flight attendant informed me I had poured water on the crotch of the man seated next to me and told everyone he had pissed his pants.

I like licking my own skin and then blowing it dry with my breath because it creates a vinegary smell that I find appealing. I tend to do this in Teams calls without knowing it, but someone recently told me they've seen me doing it and asked me could I stop.

Today, we ran out of loo roll in the downstairs toilet. Didn't realise until I'd dropped the kids off at the pool. Had to hobble into kitchen with pants round knees and wipe my arse with a slice of bread.

I blocked the bog with a massive turd at my girlfriend's parents' house. So I scooped it up and lobbed it out the window. When I came downstairs, everyone was in the conservatory, looking up at the fruit of my labours.

Ninth Commandment

Thou shalt always

Laugh

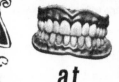

at

Yourself

and

others

It's extremely British to laugh at oneself.
While stealing stuff from Asda, naturally.

Accidentally texted a colleague that I 'needed a good seeing-to' on Friday night. I can't bear to see him at work tomorrow so I think it's best if I resign and go work in a different country.

RT: 47 FAV: 3,613

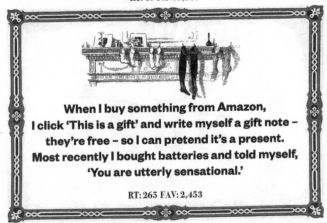

**When I buy something from Amazon,
I click 'This is a gift' and write myself a gift note –
they're free – so I can pretend it's a present.
Most recently I bought batteries and told myself,
'You are utterly sensational.'**

RT: 265 FAV: 2,453

I got told that your tongue is never in a comfortable position, Every now and then I remember, and it takes me a few minutes to forget. The wife keeps asking me what I'm thinking about but I can't tell her, she already thinks I'm an idiot.

RT: 246 FAV: 3,972

I'm So British It Hurts

Are you the type of person who apologises to a door when you walk into it? Welcome to Britain, you'll be sorry to leave.

~~~~

**When I wander round a shop and then leave
without buying anything, I walk out extra slowly
to demonstrate I haven't nicked anything.**

RT: 187 FAV: 4,252

My hair never gets out the same way, despite me going to the same place every time, with the same person & asking for the same thing. They're shit, but I'm too British to say and too lazy to go anywhere else.

RT: 6 FAV: 218

I saw my neighbour gardening and congratulated her on her pregnancy. Turns out she wasn't pregnant. Put my house on the market the next day; it seemed the only decent thing to do.

RT: 145 FAV: 3,448

Our cleaner is so useless that we pay a second cleaner to come when she is gone. We can't bring ourselves to sack the first one, as she's just a really nice lady.

RT: 163 FAV: 2,675

I'm so British that when I was 19, a woman I had spent the entire night talking to invited me inside her flat for a cup of tea and I genuinely thought all she wanted was tea. We drank tea until 6 in the morning, at which point I was tired and went home. Nothing else happened.

RT: 288 FAV: 4,003

LAUGHING AT YOURSELF

On a bus once, a lady pressed the bell but it didn't ring. So I pressed the one near me for her. She then realised it wasn't her stop, so stayed on. But I'd rung the bell and everyone saw me do it. So I had to get off rather than be embarrassed at having wasted everyone's time.

RT: 341 FAV: 6,012

Classic situation with my neighbour knowing my name and me not having a clue about his. Rather than be an adult about it, I've paid £3 for a copy of the land registry title plan just to get his name. Cheers, Martin.

RT: 300 FAV: 3,969

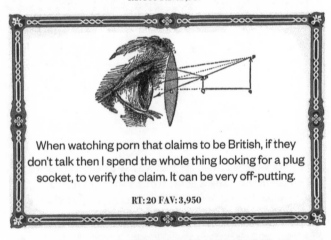

When watching porn that claims to be British, if they don't talk then I spend the whole thing looking for a plug socket, to verify the claim. It can be very off-putting.

RT: 20 FAV: 3,950

I sucked off a tramp out of politeness.
An uber-drunken ex woke me early one morning with a man he'd 'picked up' for a threesome. Said man was clearly a vagrant. Ex passed out. I felt bad & rather British about the whole shebang. Showered, fed, blew him & sent him off with change.

RT: 12 FAV: 261

I once walked into a pub toilet and saw a geezer shitting in the urinal. I didn't know how to act so did the awkward British 'Alright, mate.'

I'm so British that I occasionally say thank you to my Glade Sense & Spray air freshener when it goes off.

Whimsical Thoughts and Behaviour

Whimsy is what it means to be British.
That and invading half the globe.

~~~~

When I am walking my dogs on a cold morning, I like to take a hip flask of whisky and drink some, pretending I am a cop from the 70s on a stake-out trying to keep warm, rather than a borderline alcoholic.

Drivers think I'm saying thank you when they stop for me at a zebra crossing, but really I'm pretending to use The Force to stop their car.

I like to ring the phone number of the house I grew up in and ask to talk to myself. 'He doesn't live here anymore.' 'Oh,' I reply, disappointed.

When it rains, I deliberately walk around with my shoelaces untied so that I can pretend to be tying them when I'm really rescuing worms, but am too embarrassed to admit it.

RT: 160 FAV: 2,236

I park the forklifts at work next to one another at the weekend so they don't get lonely.

RT: 364 FAV: 7,900

Whenever I have a drink straight from the tap, I put my hands behind my back and pretend I'm Liam Gallagher. LG x.

RT: 328 FAV: 5,671

I've been trying to set up two of my friends for a while, inviting them both to events so they can meet up. They have nothing in common, but her surname is Merry and his is Christmas. It's my mission to get them married and create the ultimate double-barrelled festive surname.

RT: 290 FAV: 5,809

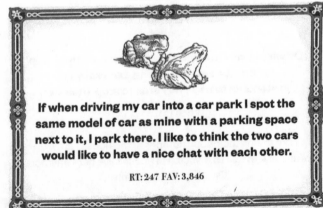

If when driving my car into a car park I spot the same model of car as mine with a parking space next to it, I park there. I like to think the two cars would like to have a nice chat with each other.

RT: 247 FAV: 3,846

When I delivered papers in the early morning in the snow,
I'd walk backwards to random people's front doors, then
follow my steps back out. Imagine people's faces when they
leave for work & think that someone's already left their house.

RT: 82 FAV: 2,726

**When I'm in the park, I like to give the squirrels
Hobnob biscuits. They hold them in both paws and turn
them to nibble at the edges. I think it makes them look
like furry truck drivers and it makes me happy.**

RT: 225 FAV: 5,009

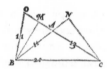

I am the Master
of Technology

*No one knows how technology works anymore. Blame iPhones.
Once it became all fingers stabbing at a screen, no one
could be bothered learning stuff anymore.*

I have absolutely no sense of direction. When using Google
Maps, I just have to start walking to see if my 'dot' is going
in the right direction. Sometimes this takes more than
4 attempts as I can't remember the streets I've already tried.

RT: 933 FAV: 13

**I feel low-level shame and embarrassment when
MS Word can't even work out what word I've tried to spell.**

RT: 153 FAV: 2,676

LAUGHING AT YOURSELF

Fixed my mum's iPad and linked hers and mine together somehow. Everything I did appeared on her iPad. The final straw was when I was watching some piss porn – she had to ring me and asked me to stop as it was getting too much. Very bad times.

RT: 188 FAV: 3,797

When I'm doing the laundry, I always assure my wife that I've done it on the necessary settings depending on what's going in. Bollocks. Same temperature, spin and programme, regardless of what's in there.

RT: 176 FAV: 2,871

'I can't wait for you to fuck my arse and for me to cum on your chest while you wank me' was the WhatsApp I accidentally sent to my dad instead of a guy called Dave.

RT: 314 FAV: 3,446

I once got so stoned I watched an entire movie on mute & cried because I thought I'd gone deaf.

RT: 679 FAV: 14.8K

Bought a dishwasher with a silver front on it and had it delivered. It was only when I opened it that I saw it was gold-fronted. I was angry, but wasn't worth the hassle of waiting for a replacement. A year later, I realised it was silver with gold protective wrap I'd never removed.

RT: 308 FAV: 112

My husband wasn't home, so as I had the house to myself, I decided to watch some porn and enjoy some alone time. Midway through, the sound disappeared on the video and I couldn't figure it out. My phone had connected to the Bluetooth in my husband's car when he got home.

Alcohol – I Rue the Day I Met You

We have a terrible relationship with booze in Britain, largely because the pubs are shut for 10 miserable hours.

~~~~

As a teenager, I stole Baby Jesus from the nativity scene at the Guildhall and rode down a main road with it drunk in a shopping trolley. It was in the paper and was a big whodunnit type affair. Nobody knows who took it to this day. It was me. I stole Jesus. He's in the canal.

LAUGHING AT YOURSELF

I was 16 or 17 and got home very drunk. So drunk,
in the night I pissed in the corner of my bedroom.
In the morning my mum saw and smelled it and
went crazy. I quickly pissed in her bedroom, too,
without her seeing, then blamed the dog.
The dog was never allowed upstairs again.

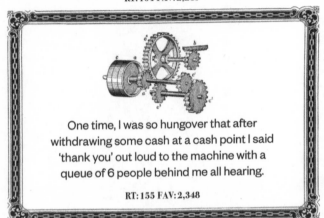

One time, I was so hungover that after
withdrawing some cash at a cash point I said
'thank you' out loud to the machine with a
queue of 6 people behind me all hearing.

Many years ago, I drove horribly drunk because a girl
I met in a club said I could have anal sex with her if
I took her home. I was so pissed I drove over one of those
massive roundabouts on a major road. I still feel guilty
for the people I could have killed. Worth it, though.

Met a girl at a club, went back to hers for some action.
Couldn't cum 'cos I was too pissed, so thought I'd try doing
a little wee in her instead and claim I'd finished. In trying to
push a wee out, I shat the bed instead. Never saw her again.

One night I got so drunk I fell asleep on the toilet. Waking up, I took my shoes off to creep into the bedroom so as not to disturb my wife and found myself standing in the public bar of my local with a shoe in each hand.

I think smoking is absolutely horrible and anyone who smokes is a victim of the tobacco industry. Until I've had three pints, then I basically turn into Serge Gainsbourg and can't get enough of the delicious little bastards.

At the train station, and the train wasn't due to arrive for 30 minutes. I was annoyed and hungover. I sat alone on the platform, staring at the tracks. A man approached me and asked if I was OK and said things will get better. Not suicidal mate, just hungover, but thanks for the concern.

New to London from NZ, I caught a late train home to Clapham after a big night out. I fell asleep & was kicked out at the last stop. I didn't recognise the station, so opened Google Maps. My eyes widened as I kept having to zoom out. And that's how I learned where Southampton is.

LAUGHING AT YOURSELF

**Boozy walking holiday one hot summer,
I woke up naked in the tent with a mad thirst.
I streaked down to the stream for a drink.
The Labrador's nose in my arse alerted me to the
dog-walker. 'Morning' she said as I looked up from
drinking the river like a recently turned werewolf.**

Ludicrous Misapprehensions That I've Had

*Your editor once believed that Liverpool would have
a large pool with livers in it. He was six at the time,
but still hasn't visited to check.*

~~~~

Until I saw Blur in Hyde Park in 2009 and
until the guy from *Quadrophenia* came on stage,
I believed Paul Daniels did the talky bits in 'Parklife'.

**I once got a 'Caesar cut' from my Polish barber. I quite
liked the style and kept asking for it every single time
I went back. 3 years and a change of barber later,
I realised I'd just heard 'scissor cut' with an accent.**

For nearly a decade, I have been telling people – when appropriate, not randomly – that I have a retrofitted uterus. My doctor finally corrected me this week: retroverted.

I was 42 when an 8-year-old told me a pony wasn't a baby horse.

I genuinely used to think that the speed at which the New Scotland Yard sign turned was dependent on the severity of the crimes taking place at that time. The worse the crimes, the faster it turned.

At the age of 38, I discovered that the word 'segue' was not spelled 'segway' and that the word 'segue' was not pronounced 'seeg'. I have a PhD.

I was in my late 20s when I discovered that not getting my cycling proficiency when I was 12 didn't mean I wasn't allowed to cycle down the high street.

Until my mid-30s, I thought that the 'No return within 1 hour' on parking signs meant that once you'd parked, you weren't allowed to come back to your car for at least an hour.

RT: 477 FAV: 109

I spent a bit of the 90s wondering what a dord was and why the Stone Roses wanted to be one.

RT: 541 FAV: 4,922

For years, I was under the impression that '*Mein Führer*' meant 'motherfucker' in German. I'd say it frequently at work when I'd make a small mistake or at soccer when I'd miss a chance. It turns out I was mistaken and that many people have due reason to assume I'm a Nazi.

RT: 236 FAV: 5,479

Let's All Revel in Being Lazy Arses, Shall We?

~~~~~~

Never do today what you can put off to tomorrow and eventually never do at all, because oops, Nan is dead now and doesn't need a Christmas card.

~~~~

The TV went into standby mode about an hour ago. I have sat in silence since as I'm too lazy to get up and find the remote.

RT: 84 FAV: 1,598

When I'm feeling really lazy and can't be bothered to go down to the office kitchen, I cut my Scotch egg in half with a ruler.

RT: 158 FAV: 2,154

I just printed an empty page at work because I was too lazy to bend over and take one out of the printer tray.

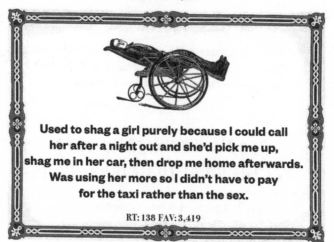

Used to shag a girl purely because I could call her after a night out and she'd pick me up, shag me in her car, then drop me home afterwards. Was using her more so I didn't have to pay for the taxi rather than the sex.

I've spent a fortune on a turntable, amp and speakers. After a short spell buying vinyls, old and new, I can't be arsed to get out of my chair to turn the record over and now just stream music on Spotify instead.

I was self-employed for about 4 years. I never once paid tax. Not because I am an asshole, but because I couldn't work out how to do it.

My wife works in the public eye. I use her Wikipedia page to make sure I don't forget her birthday or our wedding anniversary. I should be ashamed, but I'm not.

LAUGHING AT YOURSELF

I'm due to get married in a month. I don't even think I like him anymore, but can't be arsed with the hassle of moving his furniture out of our flat.

RT: 396 FAV: 3,666

People Who Rightly Have Not Let Go of Their Inner Child

~~~~~~

Your inner child probably wants to shit themselves. Do it.

~~~~

Police pulled me over and asked why I was driving up and down the road late at night. I came clean and explained my mileage was 80 thousand and 84 miles and I needed 1 more mile to make 80085, i.e. BOOBS.

RT: 508 FAV: 116

I will not leave my local swimming pool until they have put on the wave machine. I even ask the lifeguards when they're switching it on. I'm 45.

RT: 106 FAV: 3,597

I'm a grown man who sits at the front seat on the top deck of the bus so children can't. The look on their stupid faces when they see me, a grown adult, living their dream.

RT: 227 FAV: 4,333

I'm 32 years old and still argue with children online over _FIFA_. Recently I screenshotted my bank balance to win an argument with what turned out to be a 12-year-old. That'll learn him.

RT: 350 FAV: 6,486

Sometimes when I see my postman approaching, I crouch by the letterbox, snatch the letters as they are posted and bark like an angry dog. I don't have a dog and I'm pretty sure my postman knows that. I'm 50.

RT: 263 FAV: 6,749

I'm a private tutor and one day one of my students, 7, showed me his new remote-controlled Lego buggy. I, 36, was so envious that I went home and sheepishly asked my wife if I could buy some Lego. She said yes. I bought the exact same set and I couldn't be happier.

RT: 380 FAV: 19

At the supermarket, I still like to glide on my trolley, skimming the ground with my feet like a serene spaceman. I'm nearly 50.

RT: 259 FAV: 5,133

Wanking Anxiety and Other Modern Superstitions

Honestly, this section is mostly about wanking.
Sorry about the wanking, Mum.

~~~~

I can't have a wank if the Henry hoover is in the same room. It's like he's looking at me.

RT: 222 FAV: 2,624

I haven't had a wank since my mum passed away last June.
I'm scared her ghost will catch me cracking one off.

RT: 181 FAV: 2,252

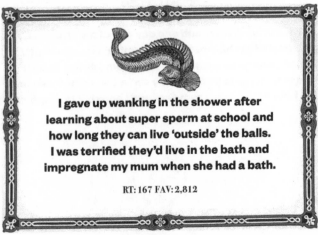

I gave up wanking in the shower after learning about super sperm at school and how long they can live 'outside' the balls. I was terrified they'd live in the bath and impregnate my mum when she had a bath.

RT: 167 FAV: 2,812

When my girlfriend goes for a shower in the morning
she puts the cat on the bed, because she thinks it will
stop me wanking if the cat's watching. It doesn't.

RT: 196 FAV: 2,518

I've inherited a beautiful signet ring that's been passed down the generations from 18th-century aristocracy. However, whenever I have a wank, I can't help but think about my dad, who must have also wanked wearing the ring. It's not ideal.

Growing up, I loved the *Toy Story* franchise and now my young kids have *Toy Story* toys. One toy broke and I couldn't throw it away due to the profound impact of the films, so I've hidden it in the loft with another toy to keep it company.

Whenever I'm looking for a new car, I always do it out of earshot of my current car. I feel if my current car hears my plans, it will play up and become a fucker to sell.

Whenever I leave the house for an extended period of time – weekend away etc. – I film myself locking the front door in case I wake up in a panic I hadn't locked it.

My dad was a vicar and his most beloved possession is a vial of water from some well in the Bible. As a kid, I didn't want my cat to go to hell, so I used the vial of water to baptise him, then replaced it with tap water. Dad cherishes the vial of tap water to this day.

LAUGHING AT YOURSELF

The Day I Realised I Was Fat

We are body-positive at Fesshole Towers, and the four chins we can see reflected in the laptop screen as we type this all agree.

~~~~

I have put on so much weight in the last 2 years,
I've gone up a shoe size.

RT: 104 FAV: 2,858

**I'm so greedy that sometimes if we order takeaway,
I'll add extra sides and then pretend to my
wife that the restaurant gave them to us for free
or that the app 'must have broken'.**

RT: 47 FAV: 2,076

When phoning for a takeaway, I'll often ask the restaurant to
hold on while I check the order is correct with my friends.
I'm not checking. There is nobody else. I'm a fat bastard.
I just don't want the takeaway to know.

RT: 393 FAV: 6,673

**Driving back from the Chinese takeaway, the order was
sitting on the passenger seat & it was so heavy it set off
the seatbelt warning noise. It was only for me.**

RT: 199 FAV: 5,888

We bought a fancy new oven with a touch panel last year.
Now, when I'm cooking on the hob and lean over to
give the pan a stir, my belly switches the oven on.
My old oven never used to troll me like this.

RT: 38 FAV: 2,395

We've banned Peppa Pig from the house, because she's naughty for the sake of being naughty and thus a bad role model. However the real reason I supported this banning is that as I'm fat, middle-aged, wear glasses and work in IT, I'm Daddy Pig's double.

RT: 245 FAV: 8,372

Your Nicknames for People

~~~~~~

You shouldn't give nicknames to people behind their backs as invariably it'll get back to them and make you look bad. Like that time we spotted the neighbour eating two burgers at McDonalds and started calling them 'two burgers'. Sorry, Carol.

~~~~

I've secretly named the colleagues in my department as follows: Sour Cow, Bearded Slaphead, Golf Cunt, Obvious Rug, Still Here Somehow, The Banter Twat Brothers, Vegetable Breath, Blew David At Xmas, Smiling Weirdo, Toilet Noises, Sexual Malcolm, Arseface.

RT: 791 FAV: 5,250

I make up names for all the other parents on the school run. So far, there is Guppy-faced Woman, Trophy Wife, Peter Jones's Little Brother, Ursula, Pea Eyes, Stick Insect, Weirdy Beardy, Trout Face and Captain Caveman. I don't speak to any of them and nobody knows.

RT: 363 FAV: 4,552

I call my father-in-law 'Brains'. My wife thinks it is because I think he is smart. It's not, it's because he walks like a Thunderbird.

RT: 42 FAV: 2,462

We used to call a guy at work TC, which he liked because he thought it was short for Top Cat, when actually it was short for That Cunt.

RT: 311 FAV: 5,197

Celebrity Bin

~~~~~~

Fesshole is about the public, not those celebrities that suck up the oxygen of the entire public discourse. However that doesn't mean you don't send in stuff about celebs – we could probably run our own hooky version of Popbitch this way.

~~~~

I've developed an obsession with Jimmy Nail & fantasise about being with him. Being a happily married lesbian, I'm not sure how to process this.

RT: 247 FAV: 2,205

Used to live in George Michael's old house from his Wham! days. Address must have been online somewhere as we'd receive about 5 begging requests for autographs each week. We'd sometimes send one, but sign as 'George Michel' to fuck with the eBay sellers.

In 2007, my then-girlfriend had a flat in London in which you couldn't get from the bed to the bathroom without passing some giant windows. One morning while hungover on the way to the loo, I saw Neil Kinnock moving in to the house opposite. I did a naked dance until he saw me.

I made Michael Portillo change his after-dinner speech by telling him the entire audience had already heard him last week. In reality no one had apart from me. I just didn't want to hear the same anecdotes. He spent the next hour frantically thinking of new material.

I had a skiing lesson with Eddie the Eagle and he told me I wasn't very good. A bit rich, mate.

When I was 8, I spent many hours on writing a letter to get on to television. I wrote in my best handwriting, and added glitter and sequins. The letter was never answered. At the time, I was heartbroken, but looking back, I am glad Jimmy Savile didn't fix it for me to dress as Barbie.

LAUGHING AT YOURSELF

Was late for a train and this old man was just ambling down the corridor at my work. Pushed past him, muttering, 'Silly old sod.' Then noticed a film crew at the end of the corridor filming a bemused Melvyn Bragg, who I'd just shoved out of the way.

RT: 89 FAV: 2,509

I always line the cat-litter tray with the free local paper. Before I lay it down, I fold it so local MP Liam Fox is face-up for the cats to do their business on him. It's the small things.

RT: 195 FAV: 4,290

Deborah Meaden once asked me for directions, and I sent her the wrong way on purpose because I didn't like her *Dragon's Den* persona. Every time I see her tweeting on the right side of things, I feel more guilty. I haven't blocked or muted her, though, as I deserve it. Soz Deb.

RT: 81 FAV: 2,919

I once pissed all over my hand on purpose and didn't dry it off until after I'd shaken Nigel Farage's at a meet-and-greet.

RT: 222 FAV: 1,674

Monumental Embarrassment

~~~~~~

People who need to move to a different country to cope with it all.

~~~~

My wife thinks we moved house because I wanted
a bigger garden. In reality, my neighbour overheard me on
a sex chat line and I couldn't face the embarrassment.

RT: 1,038 FAV: 2,022

**I once reported my wallet lost to police only to later find
it under the driver's seat. I tossed it in a river to avoid
the embarrassment of telling my husband this.**

RT: 12 FAV: 585

Lodged with an old couple in Birmingham a few years ago.
Dave and Barb. Salt of the Earth. Cheap rent, tiny house,
so ate together, watched TV, etc. After 6 months I left.
'Bye Dave!' I said as we hugged. 'It's Pete,' he whispered.
'Dave, why didn't you tell me?' I shouted.

RT: 165 FAV: 5,109

**My girlfriend and I went to Glastonbury. Invested in
the whole lot. Wheelbarrow. Tent. Wooden spoon-
making. On Friday the mud was getting too much.
Saturday morning, we packed up and went home.
Too embarrassed to tell any of our friends, so we
stayed off social media and ordered delivery.**

RT: 108 FAV: 2,061

My daughter Lily's piano teacher misheard her name when she first started lessons and we didn't correct her at the time. Now it's gone on so long we're both too embarrassed to tell her. So, next month, Milly will be giving her first-ever piano recital.

One of my neighbours pops round every 3 months or so to tell me he's going on holiday and to give me a key in case of emergency. He collects it 2 weeks later and gives me a bottle of wine. I have no idea who he is or where he lives.

I'm a 40-year-old male and often go for months without cutting my toenails until they resemble claws. A few months, ago I twisted my ankle at work and the first-aider removed my sock in front of the whole office. Been looking for a new job since; can't live with the embarrassment.

My flat got burgled years ago. I went to the police station to give them a list of the items stolen, which included my MiniDisc Walkman. While there, I put my hand in my coat pocket and found it. Never mentioned it out of embarrassment.

I'm not good with kids. I worry my awkwardness around them could be misconstrued as me being a massive paedo. I once tried to smile at a toddler on the bus, and then spent the rest of the day worrying I'd be on *Crimewatch*.

RT: 52 FAV: 2,815

Things I Used to Believe as a Child

The main thing you should believe as a young person is that life is fair, so that adulthood can be a crushing disappointment that the entire system is fixed.

~~~~

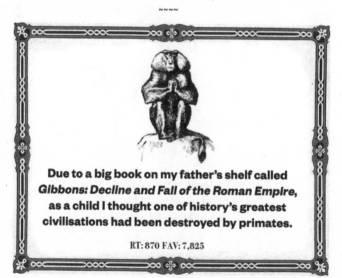

Due to a big book on my father's shelf called *Gibbons: Decline and Fall of the Roman Empire*, as a child I thought one of history's greatest civilisations had been destroyed by primates.

RT: 870 FAV: 7,825

As a child, I used to think that the death penalty meant that someone would take a penalty and if they scored, the person would live.

RT: 232 FAV: 4,077

When I was a kid, I thought the name Barry was short for Barold, as in Harry & Harold. Only learned it wasn't the case when my teacher called me a stupid fool in front of class for mentioning it.

RT: 408 FAV: 3,848

I refer to Dennis the Menace's dog as Ganasher – no silent G. I didn't know about silent Gs when I was 9, and at 47 I'm not changing.

RT: 129 FAV: 5,041

As a child, I was terrified that someone being ostracised meant they slowly turned into an ostrich.

RT: 271 FAV: 3,472

When I was little, I used to think it was compulsory to go on *Blankety Blank* as a contestant. I thought it was like jury service and I would lie awake at night worrying about being called up.

RT: 255 FAV: 3,337

As a kid, I wanted to be a bin man because I thought they only worked one morning a week. Little did I know the other 4 days they collected other area's bins.

RT: 211 FAV: 5,946

When I was a kid, I used to think that you were given a young-sounding name when you were born, something like Ben, but when you became an old man, you had to change it to something like Arthur or Seth.

RT: 229 FAV: 4,544

As a child, our house got burgled on the millennium NYE. CSI came in to dust for fingerprints and I ran away from home, because I knew my prints would be on everything and I had accepted I was going to jail. I lived in the house and I was 11.

RT: 75 FAV: 4,866

At 6, I went to Spain with my mum, dad and older brother. I'd been swimming for ages. Dad said I'd shrink if I stayed in too long. A few hours later, I got changed and my underpants kept falling off. I cried and screamed, thinking I'd shrunk. Turns out they were my brother's underpants.

RT: 167 FAV: 4,752

When I was little, I made a wish to be a Labrador puppy. After noticing blond hairs on my arms I thought it was coming true and cried myself to sleep for several nights, thinking about how cross my mum and dad would be.

RT: 309 FAV: 9,377

LAUGHING AT YOURSELF

I Am an Idiot

~~~~~~

If there's one thing British people like to admit,
it's to being absolute numbskulls. Glory be to these sweet idiots.

~~~~

I kept rejecting Netflix films suggested by my wife as they
were always rated at a lowly 5.1. It was only recently
I realised that the number refers to the surround sound.

RT: 162 FAV: 5,593

**I am 54 and recently had chest pains. I went to A&E and
had an ECG. All clear. Had a conversation with the senior
nurse to try and ascertain what the cause may have been.
We concluded that I had probably eaten too much cheese.**

RT: 325 FAV: 6,535

Years ago, my skin turned a faint blue tinge one day.
I was rushed to hospital as it's a symptom of cyanosis,
which can be very serious. After hours of tests which
stumped doctors, it turned out it was fabric dye rubbed
off on to my skin from my brand-new blue bed sheets.

RT: 128 FAV: 2,987

I had a job interview and during small talk complimented them on their decor. I got a rejection from them almost immediately. They said they needed someone who could tell the difference between a Zoom background and reality.

I went to a conference where there was a little goody bag for each delegate. Inside the bag, among other things, was a fizzy sherbet-type sweet, which I duly attempted to eat. It was a bath bomb.

Took my cat to the vet because I was concerned about some lumps I'd found on him. Paid £32 to have the vet tell me that my cat did indeed have nipples.

For the last 8 months, I've thought I was a naturally talented piano player. Turns out my child's toy piano plays a specific song no matter which keys you press. I found this out at a friend's house on a real piano.

Hungover and running late for work, phone sandwiched between ear and shoulder, coffee in hand, I reached into my bag for my Oyster card. Repeatedly tapped the card with no luck, until I looked down and saw I was using an Always Ultra.

LAUGHING AT YOURSELF

I'm not really into gadgets but my wife convinced me to get a pair of AirPods. I didn't think I'd need the 'plastic case' they came in so threw it away. After I realised what it was for, I was too embarrassed to tell her and said I lost it.

RT: 117 FAV: 4,217

Filling in a blood donor questionnaire once, I got denied because I admitted to having sex in Africa. I had been visiting Kenya with my wife; I didn't realise it meant the sex had to be with the locals.

RT: 69 FAV: 6,840

I had a dream last night about a great new podcast. I woke up to write it down for the morning, then went back to sleep. Woke up this morning to see what amazing idea I had: Paranormal Rice.

RT: 234 FAV: 4,091

Hoist With My Own Petard

~~~~~~

Here's a fact, so you learn one thing from this terrible book: a 'petard' is a small explosive, so being hoist with it means your own bomb lifted you clean in the air.

~~~~

I created a time capsule in lockdown and decided to put my spare car key in there so future people could see what a car key was, as all cars will be keyless, I assume? Needless to say, I had to dig it up last week as I lost my original key and now my garden's a mess.

RT: 234 FAV: 7,981

I stole a poster catalogue from the National Gallery.
I couldn't believe they had the gall to charge £2.50 for it,
so walked out with it brazenly thinking that if I was stopped
I would just say I thought it was free. I wasn't stopped
but when I got home, we'd been burgled.

**One Xmas I decided to get my girlfriend jewellery
and so I got her a necklace and a ring.
She opened the ring, burst into tears, said
'yes' and phoned her parents to say
we're engaged. I couldn't break her heart.
Been unintentionally married for 10 years.**

I ran a marathon. About 3 miles from the finish line,
I was struggling and needed a distraction. So I ran
behind a random woman, just concentrating on her ass.
Got to the finish line and overtook her. It was an old guy.

**I have never been to Nando's. I let people know that
I have never been to Nando's and never will go
to Nando's because it's overpriced KFC. Secretly,
I would love to go to Nando's, but I can't turn back now.**

LAUGHING AT YOURSELF

When I was 11, I faked a sore tummy to get out of going to school – I was dreading a drama skit thing. I ramped up my complaints over the weekend. On Monday my mum kept me off school and took me to the GP, who sent us straight to the hospital, where I had my appendix removed.

RT: 438 FAV: 122

I'd saved nearly £5k over many years in a separate bank account as a safety net for when I inevitably leave my husband – he found a paper statement I'd stupidly left out over Christmas and I panic-lied and said it was for a luxury holiday. He is thrilled, I am bereft.

RT: 529 FAV: 6,062

My wife wanted a threesome, with another man. I found a bloke online, we all met, hit it off and had several sessions. She begged me to allow her to play solo, and I agreed. 6 months on, he's living in my house, she's pregnant with his kid and I'm in a bedsit.

RT: 322 FAV: 255

At our wedding, we decided to place the two most argumentative people we know on the same table. Sadly this didn't create the hilarity we expected and they are now very close friends.

RT: 36 FAV: 492

I got mugged by a gang in Paris. I thought I'd get away with it by acting confused and telling them in broken French that I only speak English, but they just mugged me in English instead.

RT: 263 FAV: 4,438

I hated my ex-neighbour so much I used to call him 'FUCKING BRIAN' under my breath every time he walked past our house. One time we were in the supermarket and so was he. We said hello, and my then 5-year-old said 'Mum, is that fucking Brian?'

RT: 191 FAV: 5,114

I was working away and told my girlfriend I had a surprise for her on Friday night when I got back. She got it into her head I was going to propose and invited loads of friends round. A surprise new dishwasher was not appreciated.

RT: 187 FAV: 4,645

I've been a vicar in a small, quintessentially English village for 16 years. I love the village fêtes, chatting to people in the community and giving out advice whenever I'm asked. There's only 1 problem... I don't believe in God.

RT: 371 FAV: 2,639

Moments of Realisation
That This Is It,
This Is Your Life

Burroughs states in his introduction to Naked Lunch*: 'The title means exactly what the words say: naked lunch, a frozen moment when everyone sees what is on the end of every fork.'*

~~~~

I regularly go into Greggs for breakfast. I despise the human sputum that congregate in these places and regularly sneer at these lowlifes as I enjoy my morning coffee. However, I recently clocked myself in the window's reflection on the way out and realised I am I one of them.

RT: 148 FAV: 2,961

Every one of my exes has gone on to meet the love of their lives right after me – always genuinely fantastic people, often extremely intelligent and kind. Meanwhile, I'm having to face the fact that I may well be the problem.

RT: 280 FAV: 4,884

My favourite part of the day is driving to and from work because
it's the only part of the day that I'm not at home or work.

RT: 120 FAV: 2,743

**I've been utterly besotted by a taken man for most of
my adult life. Knew nothing would ever happen but still
fantasised. He recently used 'holibobs' in a text
and I am finally, mercifully, 100% cured.**

RT: 623 FAV: 23.4K

Now that I finally have money to buy console games,
I'm too old to enjoy them anymore. I'm gutted.

RT: 346 FAV: 3,702

**Things with my husband are fine enough, but
I secretly hope that he splits up with me so that he can
have the kids every other weekend and a couple of
nights in the week so I can have time to myself again.**

RT: 144 FAV: 2,370

I was a heavy weed smoker for 20 years.
I stopped 2 years ago and since then I've fallen
out with half the people I know. Not the weed's fault,
I've just realised what absolute horrors they were.

RT: 103 FAV: 4,383

LAUGHING AT YOURSELF

I do 95% of the cooking and cleaning in our household. My wife thinks it's because I want to break down gender stereotypes for our kids but in truth, she's shit at both and I want to eat nice dinners and live in a clean house.

RT: 277 FAV: 7,102

I once took my kids to Kew Gardens and they made up an annoying song that they sang continuously until I got grumpy. Now they're grown up that memory breaks my heart – I got grumpy about a song on a day we'll never get to do again. What a massive bellend. Savour every moment.

RT: 420 FAV: 11.9k

I put off really easy, simple tasks at work for no reason. Sometimes I'll literally be sweating from anxiety because it becomes such a huge weight on my back. Then at the last minute I'll do it and feel so silly. I do this at least once a week.

RT: 453 FAV: 8,536

Stood in B&Q with a load of paint and rollers etc. I looked eyes with another bloke at the next till with a similar stack of crap. Both of us stood next to our chatterbox wives. At that moment, we shared an unspoken 'Shit this, isn't it?' look. A brief smile and we parted ways.

RT: 89 FAV: 43,818

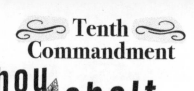

Thou shalt have a Happy heartwarming Ending

like in a Hollywood movie

Let's finish on a high – our advice is to score some heroin from that dude who hangs around the bridge on Camden Lock. No, that's hitting the wrong note, innit... Seriously, we've put heartwarming stuff at the end so you finish in a good mood. A happy finish, if you will.

**Every time I see a kid under 10ish
wearing glasses, I always say,
'Wow, I love your glasses!'
because I fucking hated wearing
glasses as a kid. I really
hope it makes their day.**

My 12-year-old son recently started to stream on Twitch.
After weeks of zero interactions, he was ecstatic
to announce that he had not only a viewer but a
follower also. I've never seen a happier human being.
I am that follower. He can never know.

**Once went to a house to fix a boiler. Young mum,
2 kids. The house was cold. Sorted the problem
quickly, no parts required. She said she had
no money, not even for food. Offered a
blow-job as payment. I refused and gave her
£20 for food. I have never told anyone.**

Simple Pleasures

Life isn't all about shitting, wanking and plotting revenge on enemies, there are joyous simple pleasures too.

~~~~

Sometimes I wrap a warm towel – straight off the radiator –
round my neck and shoulders, and stand swaying
with my eyes closed, all my cares temporarily forgotten
in a moment of pure joy better than almost any
drug I've tried, and much cheaper.

RT: 205 FAV: 4,521

**Sometimes after a few beers, I lift the dog up on to the table
and hold up his chin and tail and pretend we are on Crufts.**

RT: 87 FAV: 2,299

Sometimes I don't take my phone to the toilet, and for old time's
sake read the ingredients on bleach or toothpaste instead.

RT: 608 FAV: 7,466

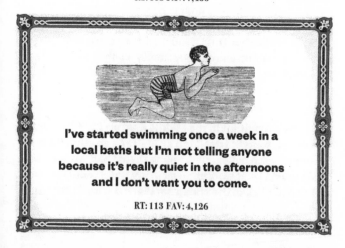

**I've started swimming once a week in a
local baths but I'm not telling anyone
because it's really quiet in the afternoons
and I don't want you to come.**

RT: 113 FAV: 4,126

HEARTWARMING

I'm 41, married with 4 kids, fit and financially secure, but the single greatest achievement of my life was last year when searching for a pair of matching socks I snapped, took out my phone and ordered a box of 200 pairs of heavy-duty PLAIN BLACK socks. Then trashed all the rest.

RT: 562 FAV: 93,439

Cycle commute went through a posh bit of town. One day, I saw a toilet being installed through a hole in the wall of a loft extension. The next day there was a window of one-way glass obscuring it from view, but for a year after, I'd look at where I knew the toilet was and wave.

RT: 81 FAV: 2,868

Sometimes when I'm in a supermarket, I can't quite believe I'm a grown-up and can buy literally anything I want in the whole shop! It makes me giddy with excitement. I'm 38.

RT: 213 FAV: 3,447

I'm a consultant in the Middle East on £250k a year tax-free; tonight I declined an invite to go out for a posh dinner with colleagues, telling them I had work to do. Actually, I just wanted to sit in my hotel room and eat Pot Noodle like the cheap northern bastard that I am.

RT: 187 FAV: 4,368

It's my day off. I found some weed in my son's bedroom this morning and smoked it in the back garden. I've been stoned off my box for two hours, and have eaten all of the cheese left over from Christmas – fucking brilliant... I'm 49. Best day off ever!

I pretend I'm presenting CBeebies _Bedtime Stories_ when I'm reading to my kids at bedtime. I put in tons of effort and imagine there's a camera in front of me and everything. At the end of each story, I look at the camera and say 'Goodnight.'

I'm 30 and like nothing better than going to the pub on my own. I'll happily sit there and have 3 or 4 pints, knowing I don't have to interact with anyone. It's absolute bliss.

I'm 37. Instead of regretting that I can't wake up age 18 again, I pretend to myself that I'm 90 and I've woken up age 37 again, and that I get to magically, wonderfully have the next 50 years again.

HEARTWARMING

People Who Love Their Kids

*We're on the home straight to the end of the book;
it's heartwarming stuff all the way.*

~~~~

At the weekend, Hubby gets up early with the children
to give me a lie-in. No point, though – the sound of the children's
laughter as he keeps them entertained means I have to get up
and join them: I know one day I'll miss that noise.

RT: 187 FAV: 6,061

**My daughter's school has a no-chocolate policy.
When she stays with me, I always put 3 or 4
Smarties loose in her lunchbox. The thought of
her excited little face furtively eating Smarties
before her teachers see makes my heart burst.**

RT: 365 FAV: 139

Both my children still need cuddles to get off to sleep. When
people ask how they're sleeping, I roll my eyes and pretend it's
really bad as they don't get themselves off to sleep or sleep
through. Secretly, I love the cuddles and never want it to end.

RT: 316 FAV: 4,547

**Two of my three children now have high sleeper
beds to give them more floor space for playing.
It breaks my heart that I can't give them a goodnight kiss
when I come upstairs to bed like I've done every other
night for the last ten years. Dad x.**

My four-year-old is my best friend. My wife thinks it's weird,
but my adult friends just sit around fucking moaning
about jobs and house prices. All my kid wants to do is
play Lego all day. I know which I'd rather do.

**When my daughter goes to bed, I play *Animal Crossing*
on her Switch for about an hour. Clean up her town, sell
fish to make her more bells. She thinks her character
is working while she sleeps. Makes her very happy.**

I'm about to become a parent for the first time.
Had to sell my nice sporty car for a more family-friendly one.
I make out like I hate my new SUV to everyone. But secretly
I love it; it's much roomier and more comfortable to drive.
I'll never admit it, though.

HEARTWARMING

My two daughters live with their mum. Every night, I message them that I love them. They get the same message, but I refuse to copy and paste as that's lazy. To make sure they know the message is written manually I make a spelling mistake in one of them every time.

Before lockdown, I was very keen to ensure I got a regular 'boys' night out' with friends. Just had our first one back and hated it. All I could think of was the two years of staying in with my wife eating takeaways in front of Netflix. I think I actually love her.

RT: 316 FAV: 14

My 10-year-old son collects unusual 50p coins but I rarely pay for anything in cash these days. To keep his collection going, I buy collectible 50ps from eBay and pretend I got given them in my change. Makes it more exciting for him.

RT: 140 FAV: 106

Sometimes from a distance I secretly watch my 2 young kids playing so they don't know I'm there. I imagine I'm now an old man and have been able to travel back in time just for this moment to see when my kids were young again. Makes me appreciate what I have right now.

RT: 219 FAV: 7,040

People Who Love Their Partners

~~~~~~

We don't want you to finish this book feeling bad about humanity. So here's some wholesome confessions so you can remember that the world isn't just full of grim bastards.

~~~~

I love my family so much; they will never know how much the family roast on a Sunday means to me. It is the best day of my life every week. I never speak of it in case this wholesome spell is broken, but I think they know.

RT: 155 FAV: 6,761

My girlfriend told me on our first date she gets excited when she finds extra fries in the bottom of the bag. Ever since, I always chuck a couple of my own in the bag when she isn't looking for her to find. The excitement she gets from it warms my heart.

My fiancée was worried about missing major milestones after she went back to work from maternity leave. Our daughter took her first steps two days ago, and I haven't told her so she still gets to see what she thinks are her first steps.

My wife is terrified of spiders and asks me throw any from the house outside. I know they'll freeze to death outside, so I just move them around the house until she sees them again. I think I've 'thrown' the same spider outside about 4 times already this week.

I bought my husband flowers today, because I was saddened to read online that men only get flowers when they die. And I thought that was pretty sad and true for most. He said he was happy because no one has ever done it for him.

**Whenever my girlfriend feels really low
and she needs someone other than me to feel better,
I always message her best mate to cheer her up.
She's convinced he's connected to her psychologically
and knows whenever she's sad. I'll never tell her,
because it makes her so happy.**

RT: 325 FAV: 116

People Who Love Their Parents

~~~~~~

*Your parents won't be around forever, you know.
Hug them if you've still got them.*

~~~~

When my mum was dying of cancer, she kept getting
upset that her daffodil bulbs weren't sprouting.
I snuck a daffodil from the park into the pot one day
while she was sleeping. She was so happy, and I'm so
glad I got to make a little magic for her before she died.

RT: 271 FAV: 21K

HEARTWARMING

People Who Love Their Neighbours

Fist bump as we sing out this book with the feel-good stuff.
Love you all.

~~~~

I'm 21 & really liked my elderly neighbour. We would chat lots and he'd invite me for Battenberg and tea. We'd watch footie and such. He died recently and I'm really sad, but I can't explain to my mates, as they thought it was weird to be friends with the old man next door.

I moved house earlier this year and my next-door neighbours, who are in their 70s, are the nicest people I've ever met. We have drinks and play darts together at least 2–3 times a week and I'm starting to worry he's becoming my best mate. I'm 24.

Just People Doing the Right Thing

Just some folks doing some good deeds and paying compliments and maybe humble-bragging about it a little – it's all good stuff that sits oddly with the stories of wanking and pissing, but it's important to have range.

~~~~

Sometimes when my girlfriend is feeling down and stuck in a loop of making herself miserable, I will deliberately misspell words when texting because she will laugh at me for being thick and it cheers her up a little.

I used to be a cleaner but I've managed to snag a good office job that requires me to travel a lot. Whenever I stay in a hotel, I always leave a sealed box of choccy biscuits behind because that shit would have made my fucking day as a depressed/stressed cleaner.

RT: 442 FAV: 21.8K

I'm 28, live on a street full of old people. My neighbour, Doris, is a lovely lady but is incredibly lonely & her memory's gone. I write postcards/bday/Xmas cards to her from made-up old people. She tells me about them over the fence with a massive smile, convinced she knows them.

RT: 263 FAV: 5,843

My neighbours are unable to afford a Wi-Fi connection and too proud to use mine. So I renamed mine Free Council Wi-Fi and told them I had read about it and what the password was. My neighbour is now halfway through an online college qualification and I'm so proud of her.

RT: 10.5K FAV: 149.6K

I used to wait tables in a chain pub. Whenever someone ordered a steak, I would ask them after their meal, 'How did you find the steak?' so that they could make the obvious joke if they wanted to. Many did. I like to think I made their day a little brighter.

RT: 225 FAV: 4,492

Before retiring last month, I was a traffic warden for 12 years. Issued thousands of parking tickets. Every single one contained a deliberate error, meaning if they challenged it, nobody would have paid a penny. You're welcome.

When tickets for big events go on sale, I add as many tickets as I can to my basket and leave them there until the basket expires and go back on sale so that people who aren't good at buying tickets can get some. It's my good deed for the week; I call myself The Ticket Picket.

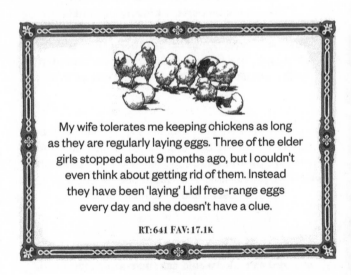

My wife tolerates me keeping chickens as long as they are regularly laying eggs. Three of the elder girls stopped about 9 months ago, but I couldn't even think about getting rid of them. Instead they have been 'laying' Lidl free-range eggs every day and she doesn't have a clue.

Why not write your <u>own</u> confessions here and then send them to someone anonymously?

_____

_____

_____

_____

_____

_____

SIX OF THE BEST COMMENTS

Twatty journalists say: 'Don't read the comments.' They are wrong, comments can be comedy gold and they're the true democracy of the internet, where you will find the best of humanity and the worst. But of course, on Fesshole, it's only the best.

~~~~

I don't know how it got into the house, but I captured a huge hornet – must have been 7cm – in a Tupperware container. Not knowing what to do with it, I stuck it in the freezer.

Hornetto.

My fiancé recently died in a routine operation. Every night I text him to tell him how much I love him. I've got his phone; I like seeing the two blue ticks like he's still alive and has read the message.

How are confessions like this on the same Twitter account as people using melon ballers to evacuate their bowels? I'm struggling to reconcile the two.

I regularly search Facebook marketplace for Sports Direct credit notes, because every now and then someone forgets to cover the codes, then I use them. I've had about £600 worth of stuff for free.

You're taking people for a giant mug.

My wife wanted a threesome, with another man. I found a bloke online, we all met, hit it off and had several sessions. She begged me to allow her to play solo, and I agreed. 6 months on, he's living in my house, she's pregnant with his kid and I'm in a bedsit.

I don't do threesomes. If I wanted to disappoint two people at once, I'd call my parents.

I'm not gay, but I did spend one week-long cycling trip shagging guys on Grindr because I didn't want to pay for hotels and needed a place to stay for the night. Would do it again.

Maybe you're bike-curious.

I'm a waitress at a venue that does at least 2 weddings a month. Over 4 years of working there, I've shagged 8 best men, 2 bridesmaids, a groom and multiple times have been offered a threesome with the married couple, but they always backed out after having a chance to sober up a bit

That's disgusting. I only hope you're not a waitresses at Josh and Katie's wedding where I'm best man at the Copthorne Hotel on July 16, 2022. Starting at 3pm. Ample parking.

Thanks to @Flannagan1992, @skimpybean, @beardySM, @billythebrit, @wattsoccuring, @Leemunden24

Here's some little hearts you can cut out and stick on your favourites – you know, like on the internet...

...and here's some common replies you can cut out and stick on your favourite confessions to simulate the entire social media experience...

Boris?

Dad?

Didn't happen.

Kitchen sofa?!

Is that actually you, Rob?

That's enough internet for me today...

Directed by Quentin Inventino

You, sir, win the internet today!

Is Tonty Blair behind this?

This is not braghole

UNFOLLOWED!

Fesshole FAQ

Is it really anonymous?

Yes, in the sense that your admin, Rob, cannot see the
email addresses or the IP addresses of who is confessing.
Google might well be tracking you, but Rob is not.

How is the blackmail side business going?

Keep up with the payments and I'll tell you.

How do I submit a confession?

Do not DM us. Do not write a message on our Facebook wall.
Do not accost us in Sainsbury's and tell us a rambling story
about shitting yourself on ketamine while we're trying to buy
a vegetarian samosa. Go here: **https://bit.ly/fessholeform**

What's the absolute worst stuff, the stuff that you don't publish?

There's a lot of men writing in to talk about wanking
on shoes and underwear. These men need to stop –
both doing this, and writing to us about it.

Have you ever felt the need to report anything to the police?

All of it.

THANKS TO...

Chris Barker for art.

Briony Gowlett for publishing.

Antony Topping for agenting.

Kat Elliott for putting up with me running terrible projects.

Stanley Manuel for being slightly impressed that @fesshole has got
half a million followers (and his old dad isn't quite so useless)

Everyone who contributed a confession –
you know who you are, and I don't because it's totally anonymous.
So I literally can't thank you by name. Sorry.

Giles Gear from Giddy Aunt Comedy
for partnering on the Fesshole LIVE! shows.

Dec Munro for crucial comedy advice: 'Don't step on the laughs'.

Hebtroco – that is, Brant Richards and Ed Oxley –
for sponsorship of the tweets.

Everyone for throwing in a few quid on KoFi
for all the endless moderation.

Plus, a few hellos to friends and family, who'll probably never see this
until they search for their own name on some archive years later –
love you good people: Max Manuel, Angus Manuel, David Stevenson,
HappyToast, Monkeon, Matt Round, Chris Shaw, John Higgs,
Kunt (and the Gang), Wil Hadden and of course Kat & Stanley again.

This book draft was written with
Python code, OCR, Google Docs & BBedit.

B3ta is still saving the web. It's the mothership. Long may she continue.

> **PEDANTS' CORNER:** The fav counts were about right in
> June 2022, but the other number is an amalgamated number
> meaning 'interactions' that adds up RTs and replies.

And remember. **FOLLOW @FESSHOLE NOW.**

FIN (shark's fin)

Fesscount: 931

 # About the Author

Rob Manuel doesn't want to be described as an author
because this book was written by the contributors,
he's more like a caretaker of an unruly mob of angry
leopards that'll eat your face off if you say the wrong thing.

He's spent his entire adult life doing exactly this in various
forms on internet projects such as B3ta.com, the much-
missed UsVsTh3m and various other social media accounts
like Anon Opin, Swear Clock and Yoko Ono Bot.

He lives in London and has one partner,
two dogs, two cats, three children and deep
anxieties about writing in the third person.

He's also available for sex work.